the macaroon bible

FROM THE FOUNDER OF DANNY MACAROONS

DAN COHEN

Photography by Alice Gao
Houghton Mifflin Harcourt
Boston • New York • 2013

This book is printed on acid-free paper.
Copyright © 2013 by Houghton Mifflin Harcourt. All Rights Reserved
Cover and Interior Photography Copyright © 2013 by Alice Gao
Interior design by Joline Rivera
Food styling by Vivian Lui
Prop styling by Kira Corbin
Published by Houghton Mifflin Harcourt
Published simultaneously in Canada.

For information about permission to reproduce selections from this book, write to Permissions, Houghton Mifflin Harcourt Publishing, 215 Park Avenue South, New York, New York 10003.

www.hmhbooks.com

Library of Congress Cataloging-in-Publication Data

Cohen, Dan, 1980-
  The macaroon bible / Dan Cohen; photography by Alice Gao.

    pages cm

  Includes bibliographical references and index.

  ISBN 978-1-118-47216-3 (cloth: acid-free paper); 978-0-544-18607-1 (ebk)

1. Macaroons. I. Title.

TX772.C3845 2013

641.86'54--dc23
                                        2012047945

Printed in China

TOP 10 9 8 7 6 5 4 3 2 1

For Evelyn

CONTENTS

ACKNOWLEDGMENTS

I'm fairly certain that I wouldn't be writing this book were it not for Morgan, whose unwavering encouragement and support from the very beginning was more valuable than words can express. Her tireless effort, sacrifice, patience, and inspiration enabled me to achieve things I never thought I'd be able to, including the creation of a chocolate malted macaroon (coming in book two!). Similarly, I'm extremely fortunate to have had the love and support of my family during the creation and growth of Danny Macaroons.

That's where it started, at home essentially, but certain other people along the way were critical in the nurturing and development of Danny Macaroons. Standing out among them are Judy Hundley and Mark Cummings of Gracious Thyme Catering. They welcomed a stranger into their kitchen and quite literally gave him the tools he needed to grow. They trusted me without knowing me, and for this I am deeply grateful. Also due thanks are Elaine, their pastry chef, who tasted and advised far more than she ever thought she would; and Ossie, Alex, and Lupe, who would often stay late so I could finish baking.

I love all of my customers, but the first major ones to take a chance on the craggy, heretofore unloved coconut macaroon, and so who now receive my most sincerest thanks, are Sheena Heisse, formerly of Gimme! Coffee; and Julie Benavides and Michael Perricone of Bergdorf Goodman. Their early faith in my product gave me encouragement and the belief in the potential of macaroons to continue onward.

Liza de Guia of the Web site and blog Food Curated, whose eye and sensitivity captured the spirit of Danny Macaroons, shared this story with many more people than I ever thought would care.

Thanks to Carla and Justin, who took a chance with a crazy person. And to Alice, Vivian, and Kira for making the macaroons in this book look so gorgeous.

And thank you to Adriana and Teresa, who have learned how to bake delicious macaroons and have enabled me to write this book and simultaneously continue to proudly provide my customers with the macaroons they love.

There is something about the richness of condensed milk, the tropical nuttiness of coconut, and the depth of vanilla that, when combined with the lightness of egg whites, work to become so much more than the constituent parts. I never really know how to explain why these cookies are so delicious, and even after hours and hours thinking specifically about this question, I still don't have any answers. The best I can say is that you just have to make them and see for yourself.

Since these are free from coconut extracts, oils, and artificial flavors, they're for coconut lovers as well as those who haven't previously liked coconut. Truly. We're so used to "coconut flavor" that few of us actually know that the flavor of real coconut is very mild. When I started Danny Macaroons, I was very reluctant to experiment with flavors. I thought that coconut had such a strong taste that there was no way that something like a Spiced Pumpkin Macaroon could work. What I eventually realized was that I wasn't thinking about what my cookie actually tasted like and was, but instead was thinking about what my cookie probably seemed like it was. Meaning: The plain macaroon is pretty mild—it tastes like toasted marshmallows (from the baked-up egg whites and sugars in the coconut and condensed milk) gently kissed with coconut. It's not overly sweetened and in your face like virtually every other coconut product on the market. It's a sturdy-but-demure, crunchy-soft pillow of comfort.

Once I started paying more attention to what this plain macaroon actually is—a wonderful canvas for creating more super-delicious macaroons—I became increasingly confident about experimenting with other flavors. This book is the result of that experimentation, fortified by more than twelve years of production and nearly three years of sales around the world—from New York to Australia to Belgium and back again.

These macaroons aren't so much coconut cookies as they are cookies that utilize coconut as the vehicle to deliver happiness to mouths. I hope you have great success in making people smile with your version of Danny Macaroons.

tools

Every job has its tool set, and delicious macaroon making is no different. The following list will help you plan out your baking so that you can create the tastiest macaroons possible.

bowls

I usually work with three bowls: a large bowl for the batter; a small bowl of water for the macaroon-forming spoons and/or your fingers; and a mixing bowl for the egg whites. The large bowl should be big enough to hold a full 14-ounce bag of coconut and to allow you to comfortably mix all of the ingredients and scoop out the macaroons. Bigger is definitely better here. The small bowl should be just large enough for you to fit your hand into—you can even use a large latte mug or one of those plastic containers wonton soup comes in when you get Chinese takeout. If you're using a handheld mixer to whip up the eggs, the bowl for the whites should be large enough to contain the resulting volume of whipped eggs.

mixer

You can use a stand mixer (with the whisk attachment) or a handheld mixer (or even a whisk if you live in the 1800s*) to whip up the egg whites. I love stand mixers because they let you work on other things while they're busy doing what they do. In practice, though, you won't see a difference in macaroons made with eggs whipped by different methods, so use whatever tool you have.

spatulas/scrapers

We're talking the silicone-topped jobbers here. They're great for mixing the coconut, scooping out the whipped whites, and folding the whites into the coconut. And for applying chocolate to the tops of macaroons (a job for which I highly recommend a spoonula). They're much easier to use for this purpose than regular spoons or spatulas/scrapers.

NOTE: For mixing the coconut, select the largest and stiffest-handled scraper you have. Flexible ends are great, but the stiffest of the soft ones are the best of the great. Wooden spoons aren't ideal, but you can certainly make do if that's what you've got.

---

*I have no idea if there were whisks in the 1800s.

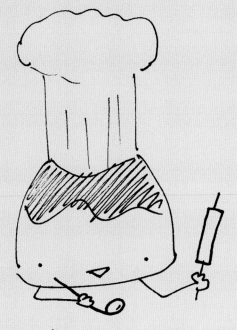

"Macaroons
ARE FUNNY LITTLE COOKIES."

teaspoons (or a large melon baller or small [1½-inch] scoop)

There are two camps when it comes to forming coconut macaroon balls: those who scrape and shape, and those who scoop. I find that it's easier to use teaspoons to shape the balls, but other people swear that it's easier to use a small scoop to dig in and then plop out the macaroon ball. I just know that I don't have small scoops sitting around my house, and that's why I learned how to do it with two teaspoons. And by teaspoons I mean: the smaller of the two that come in flatware sets; the ones you'd use to stir tea; or that kids use to eat cereal.

I should note that there is a third, fringe camp—the Handlers. Though they're largely discredited by the Macaroon Enthusiasts (ME . . .), you certainly can forego the spoons and scoops and just form the balls with your hands. Beware, though: The mixture is very sticky.

measuring spoons

You'll need a full set of measuring spoons. I prefer metal ones, but feel free to use what you've got.

baking sheets

These recipes each use a full 14-ounce bag of coconut and yield 24 macaroons that, when arranged in 4 rows of 6, happen to fit pretty nicely onto one half-sheet pan (the typical baking sheet that fits in the kind of oven you probably have in your home). I prefer baking sheets with lips on them to contain the macaroons in case some of them spread a bit too much.

cooling rack

The more wires, the better, as the macaroons have a tendency to stick a little bit to cooling racks. In the absence of cooling racks, you can always just flip the macaroons over and let them cool top down. And if you drizzle caramel on the macaroons while they're just sitting on a pan/tray/plate instead of a cooling rack, you'll get some extra bits of caramel stuck to the macaroons, which is always a good thing.

parchment or silpat

I prefer parchment paper, but if you have a Silpat (silicone mat), go ahead and use it. You can also use nonstick aluminum foil, though it doesn't work as well. Please do not use regular foil or waxed paper. If you don't have any of the first three, just spray some Pam or otherwise grease up your baking pan (and hope for the best).

kitchen scale

I couldn't possibly recommend more strongly having a kitchen scale. It's just so useful, and you wind up being more precise with your measurements. I recommend one that measures increments by the gram (or $\frac{1}{8}$ of an ounce).

techniques

Macaroons are funny little cookies. As you'll soon see, there aren't many ingredients in them, and the final product is a pretty sturdy ball of coconut bliss. But the in-between steps, while also relatively simple, can be a bit tricky to master. I've laid out some techniques that should help you bake up the macaroons of your dreams. As always, though, if you find something that works better for you, go with it. There's no "right" way to make these, no "correct" shape for them. All there is, is what you want.

whipping the egg whites

It always seems that slightly warmer eggs whip up a little nicer than slightly colder eggs, though it doesn't make a noticeable difference in the end product for these macaroons. However, two egg whites definitely take longer to whip than four.

Place your whites into the bowl, add your salt, and lower the whisk/whip into the whites. If you are fortunate enough to have a stand mixer, set it to about 60 percent of full power to whip the whites; set a handheld mixer to half power until the whites look frothy, then increase to full power. Your goal is to whip the whites until they resemble really firm whipped cream and feel firm when you touch them. This takes as long as 3 minutes. When the whipped whites pull away from the sides of the bowl, that's another good indication of when they're just about whipped enough. Note: If you get any yolk in your whites, the whites will both take longer to whip up and not whip up as stiffly.

folding the mixture

These macaroons have no leavening in them. In fact, they have pretty heavy, dense elements—coconut and condensed milk—that on their own wouldn't rise or otherwise become . . . fluffy. Enter the egg whites. All the air that was whipped into them and their firm texture will help give the macaroons a lightness and delicacy that keeps them from becoming thick, sweet, gummy balls of coconut.

However, if you dump the whipped egg whites into your coconut mixture and just stir them around, you'll deflate the eggs and defeat the entire purpose of whipping them up in the first place. So instead of mixing around in a circle, try to fold in the whites as gently as you can. Practically, this means using almost a "lift and dump" motion. Don't worry too much about breaking up the eggs, because you inevitably will, but the more careful you are, the better luck you'll have.

portioning the macaroons

Spoon or scoop, place or plop, frik or frap—everyone's got their own opinions, so my advice is to do what's comfortable for you. No matter what, if you want to make 24 macaroons out of a batch, you'll be making balls just slightly smaller than golf balls. If you decide to use the spoons, first dip them in water and shake them off, then gather some of the batter into a loose blob that seems like it'll come together to look like a golf ball. Slide it against the side of the bowl and drag it upward. Place it back down, rotated by 90 degrees, and repeat the motion, scraping and dragging it upward. Once you get a rough ball shape, you can either keep dragging to refine the shape or you can just place your ball on the baking pan by sliding the spoon out from under it. Pretend you are placing a piece of pie down on a plate; you wouldn't dump your pie off the spatula, you'd slide it off gently. Same here.

You should be able to fit 6 rows of 4 balls on your baking sheet with about an inch of space around each one. Once you've got 24 balls, you may have extra batter in the bowl. If you do, that means you made some of your balls a little too small. If you don't, and you have fewer than 24 macaroons on your pan, you made yours a little too big. If you really must have 24 macaroons, have a look over them to see if you've made ones a bit too big or a bit too small and adjust them as necessary. Dipping your fingers in your bowl of water is critical here because the batter is quite sticky. Don't worry about adding a drop or two of water to a macaroon—it won't matter. Just shake the excess water off your fingers before you handle the macaroons.

Alternatively, you can simply use your hands. Just remember to dip them in water after forming each macaroon ball; otherwise you'll have more coconut on your hands than on your baking sheet.

melting chocolate

It's easy to burn chocolate while melting it, so here are a few tips for making sure that doesn't happen. First, chop the chocolate into small, uniform pieces, which will help it melt evenly. Then, use a microwave. Place the chocolate in a microwave-safe bowl and microwave on high in 30-second increments, stirring after each increment and until the chocolate is fully melted.

If you don't have a microwave, don't worry—you can do it the old-school way. Put the chocolate in a heat-proof bowl and place over a small saucepan of gently boiling water; the bowl should form a tight seal with the pan so no steam escapes. Stir occasionally, until the chocolate is fully melted.

1. Add pure vanilla extract to the sweetened condensed milk and stir.

2. Add the coconut to the condensed milk mixture.

3. Thoroughly combine the coconut and the condensed milk mixture.

4. Whip the egg whites until very stiff peaks form.

5. Add the whipped egg whites to the coconut mixture and combine gently but completely.

6. Make the macaroon balls using two spoons.

7. Set the macaroon balls on a parchment-lined baking sheet, adjust them for size and shape if needed, and place into the oven.

8. Remove the macaroons when golden brown and beautiful.

making caramel

Ahhh caramel, the very special result of melting sugar and adding dairy. I am going to teach you how to make caramel the way I learned how to make caramel: by watching Gordon Ramsay on YouTube (true story). This is literally all I understood from his video and, as it turns out, all you really need know:

1. Put some granulated sugar in a heavy-looking pot.
2. Heat it up until it looks like the color of caramel.
3. Add your butter and stir until it's fully incorporated and looks like caramel.

That's it. No thermometer, no water, no cream, no corn syrup. (OK, OK, this is more of a toffee than a caramel. But what are we, trained chefs?) To be more explicit, though, here are some tips:

Find a pot that's the right size for the amount of caramel you want to make. You don't want too much more than ½ inch of sugar in your pot. The heavier the pot you use, the more evenly the sugar will heat and the easier it will be to control the temperature of your sugar. A thin pot is fine, but the sugar will heat very quickly and you'll have to be much more careful with it.

Put your flame on medium-high and, if you're using less than ½ cup of sugar, don't walk away. Two things may happen: The edges might melt first, and then you'll start seeing some bubbling; or the sugar might melt completely evenly (this happens most often when using just ¼ cup of sugar or a very wide pot for the amount of sugar you have) and turn yellow, then golden, then caramelly, then caramelly brown, and then dark reddish brown. Either way, cook the sugar until it's a little bit darker than you would consider to be the color of caramel. A nice deep, nutty brown. If it starts to take on a red hue, more reddish than brownish, you've gone too far. If it starts to smoke and the sugar isn't fully melted, just take it off the heat and stir, adding more heat as necessary until the sugar is fully melted. If the sugar smokes after you've already melted it all, you're dangerously close to burning it.

Add your butter and stir it up until fully incorporated. This helps stop the sugar from cooking (and makes it taste better). Add some salt and keep stirring until fully incorporated and, again, the color of caramel.

Note: The caramel gets VERY hot, a few hundred degrees or so. Please be careful with it. Careless stirring may cause splatters, and if any drops of hot caramel splatter on your skin, it'll hurt.

notes

1. Condensed milk typically comes in 14-ounce cans. Ten and a half ounces of condensed milk is about ¾ of a can or just less than 8 ounces by liquid measure.

---

2. Macaroons are TOTALLY a bake-ahead kind of cookie. I think that they're better room temperature (or cold) than they are straight out of the oven, and so if you're making these for a party, you can most definitely make them a day or two in advance, or even further ahead if you want.

---

3. Macaroons store exceptionally well in both the fridge and the freezer. If you'll be eating them within a couple of days, you can leave them out at room temperature. If you want to keep them for longer, just put them in an airtight container and stick them in the fridge (good for up to 3 weeks, depending on the flavor) or freezer (good for up to 6 months, depending on the flavor).

the history OF THE Macaroon

This is a book about delicious coconut macaroons and the things you can do with them to make them extra special. However, it's worth spending a couple of minutes going through a history of the cookie because there is a lot of confusion about what, exactly, a macaroon is; about why two very different (OK, three if we include Italian macaroons, amaretti) cookies are called the same thing; and about the origins of the cookie.

Let's start at the present: This is a book about coconut macaroons that usually look something like this and are fundamentally composed of shredded coconut, egg whites, and sugar.

Macarons, or French macaroons, usually look like this and are fundamentally composed of almond flour, egg whites, and sugar.

Italian macaroons, or amaretti, look like this and are fundamentally composed of almond flour, egg whites, and sugar.

Why are they all called "macaro(o)ns"? Because they're fundamentally the same type of cookie—a ground-nut-flour-based cookie, leavened with egg whites, sweetened, and flavored. The name is derived from the Sicilian—*maccharruni*, which were sweet and savory pastes made from different combinations of flour (wheat or nut), water, butter, and honey. Some pastes were baked as cookies, others were prepared as pastas. The word *maccharruni* comes from the verb *maccare* (to knead) and/or *ammaccare* (to crush or grind), and that's a pretty simple way to describe pastes made from ground-up wheat, nuts, or seeds.

But where do *maccharruni* come from? Not where you might have expected.

We start our consideration of the macaroon in an unlikely place: 7th century Sassanid Persia. The Persians had very tasty sweets, some of which were *faludhaj* (flour and honey confections) and *lawzinaj* (sweetened almond paste surrounded by flaky pastry). In the early half of the 7th century, Persia was invaded by the Arabs and, like all good invaders, the Arabs took note of the new and delicious foods of their newly conquered land.

Needless to say, the sweets soon spread throughout the Arab empire, which was also expanding west through northern Africa. Before too long, they found their way to Sicilian shores when the Arabs pushed north across the Mediterranean Sea.

As it often happens when different cultures mingle, recipes get shared. The Sicilians thus began to incorporate the Arabian-Persian sweets into their umbrella of *maccharruni*, and it's here that the name for a confection made from ground nuts (like sweetened almond paste) or grains began to take on its more familiar form.

At some point eggs were introduced into the recipes—for both the flour-based and the almond-based *maccharruni*—and the core ingredients of contemporary macaroons (nut flour, sugar, and eggs) have remained fundamentally unchanged since. The almond macaroons were called "amaretti," as they were made using bitter almond flour.

Amaretti are generally believed to have been introduced to France courtesy of Lorenzo de' Medici's great-granddaughter Catherine when she married King Henry II and moved to France in 1533. In French, these amaretti (really, the *maccharruni*) were translated as "macarons," for fairly obvious reasons. At around the same time, coconut was introduced to the European continent via Vasco da Gama's Indian explorations. Europeans naturally experimented with the exotic coconut, incorporating it into more and more of their dishes, and eventually ground (and shredded) coconut wound up in a macaron. As the macarons spread, their name evolved as well; in German, they were *makronen*; and, ultimately, in English, they were macaroons.

Coconut macaroons started appearing in the United States with more frequency in the 1800s and finally hit a broader market in the 1950s with the can-ification of Kosher for Passover macaroons. Why coconut macaroons for Passover instead of amaretti? Probably because they're more delicious!

The journey from a Persian almond paste treat to a fluffy, delicious coconut macaroon took quite a while. I grew up knowing macaroons as a Passover dessert but have since come to know them as a Christmas cookie, a breakfast item, a late-night treat, and a gluten-free dessert option. I think you'll join me in celebrating the truly tasty coconut macaroon's place in the dessert pantheon.

The Story of My Relationship with Macaroons and Starting the Business

The question I get asked more than any other is "Why macaroons?" As in "Why would you start a business selling macaroons when, let's be honest, most people [besides you, kind macaroon lover] don't name coconut macaroons among their favorite cookies? Plus, they only seem to appear during Passover, Christmas, and . . . well, when else DO people eat them?" The truth is that it was a complete accident. Believe me, the last thing I ever thought I'd be doing in my life was baking and selling macar—actually, no, that's the second-to-last thing I ever thought I'd do. The last thing I ever thought I'd do is bake a carrot cake macaroon and write a cookbook about it. (What was the first thing I thought I'd do? I don't know, probably be a pilot. Either that or a princess. Or maybe both at once and be known as the pilot princess.)

Growing up, my parents cooked all the time. Many of my family-related memories take place either in the kitchen or otherwise have to do with food. I always enjoyed being around food—not that I ever really helped out all that much, especially in the cleaning-up part (sorry, Mom)—and I soaked everything up like a sponge. I loved everything about the kitchen: the smells, the sounds, the tastes, the act of turning tasty things into even tastier things. As long as it was something savory. If someone was baking? Forget it, I didn't really care. And yet now I bake cookies. Go figure.

In 1999, I was studying as little as possible at Amherst College. Before I went home for Passover that year, I had a conversation with a friend about things our families eat during the holiday. He mentioned macaroons as being a dessert staple for his family that he was really looking forward to. I shrugged. Macaroons? Never really that meaningful to me.

Nevertheless, when I got home, I asked my mom why we never made macaroons. We made pretty much everything else (I suppose that by "we" I actually mean "not me"), so why not the macaroons? She shrugged (and now it's revealed that maybe I'm also a little bit of a mama's boy) and said, "I don't know, but if you want to make them, go ahead."

So I did, and that Passover my family enjoyed macaroons like never before. The next year, I was asked to make them again, and I obliged. The year after that, however, I had no interest in making macaroons again. Pigeonholing myself as the Macaroon Guy and placing the never-ending responsibility upon myself to make macaroons every. single. year. was VERY . . . unsavory. So I didn't make them. And was promptly threatened with banishment from future family gatherings if I didn't resume production.

Fast forward to 2010, and I'm at another Passover gathering, listening to and growing more embarrassed with each word as family members tell me how good the macaroons were. It was so uncomfortable—I mean, they're MACAROONS, not some fancy cake or delicate pastry. They're rough, they're not exceedingly difficult to make, they're just little cookies made up of a small handful of ingredients that I put together, mixed up, and plopped out onto a pan to bake. Nothing I understood as being especially deserving of such praise.

But my uncle's mother-in-law was particularly aggressive with her praise, telling me, over and over and over, that I should sell them, her Brooklyn-born Jewish grandmotherly accent guiltin— encouraging me into providing the macaroons to more people so they could experience what she was experiencing. I told her, as politely as possible, to leave me alone.

Two weeks later I was in a coffee shop that had outstanding coffee but no food. I asked the owners why they'd open a coffee shop without anything to eat with the coffee. They said they'd just opened and were going to figure out their food situation in the weeks to come. On the way home, something clicked in my head and I thought, "I wonder . . . if I bring them macaroons . . . if they'll give me some free coffee? Hmm."

I showed up the following week with a box of chocolate-dipped macaroons. The owners of that coffee shop looked at me understandably perplexed, wondering why I was handing them a box of macaroons. (By the way, neither of them had ever seen macaroons before.) I told them I baked them a gift for opening a great new coffee shop, and that I hoped they enjoyed them.

Their response after tasting: "Can we buy these?"

And so here we are, after almost one hundred thousand macaroons, nearly three tons (three tons!) of coconut, countless hours in the kitchen, lugging macaroons all over New York City, and trying to explain to people that yes, indeed, coconut macaroons can be really REALLY delicious. And these macaroons really ARE delicious, but they're only as delicious as you care to make them. I hope you take great joy in your macaroon creations.

The Story of the Name
It's moderately important to know that until the age of eighteen I was known as "Danny" but after that pretty much exclusively as "Dan." I just couldn't bear to introduce myself at college as "Danny"—it seemed so juvenile— and so I was "Dan." I imagine that this form of rejection of youth and desire for a seemingly more mature adulthood is pretty typical.

The way I came to be known as Danny again makes me think of Don King yelling "Only in America!" I feel like this is one of those nod-with-understanding, quintessential New York stories, and it makes me smile every time I think about it.

At the time of writing this, my production kitchen is up in Manhattan's East Harlem. A couple of avenues east of my kitchen, tucked away in Manhattan's northeast corner, is a six-block-long street called Pleasant Avenue. It is out of the way, a neighborhood unto itself possessing a history all its own and immortalized by Hollywood as the epicenter of the mid 20th century New York mafia. From Coppola to Scorsese and from Fat Tony to Johnny Roast Beef, Pleasant Avenue, whether known by name or not, is the iconic backdrop familiar to most everyone.

Things are different now. Rao's, the infamously exclusive restaurant, is the lone remaining Italian spot. The Love Café, somewhat ironically named given the street's historical reputation, is the neighborhood coffee shop. The Love Café is run by Pat Palmieri, who grew up just down the block. A neighborhood kid keeping the kinder spirit of the neighborhood alive.

On the first day I brought the macaroons anywhere, I brought them to the aforementioned coffee shop downtown and to the Love Café. I had no idea what I was doing, or if anyone would really buy them, but I had wanted to check out the café and had macaroons on me, and what else was I going to do, eat them? (And now we learn that I don't really like sweets, either.)

So I went in and asked the guy up front (who, for whatever it's worth, is named Jay, is built like a tank, and looks like he could have worked the door at some speakeasy in the '20s) for the manager (Pat). Pat emerges.

—Hi, I'm Dan, and I bake. I was wonderi—

Yeayeawhatsup?

—Well, I bake and sell to coffee sho—

OKOK, whaddya bake?

—I bake coconut macaroons. If you want, I can brin—

Whaddja say y'name was?

—Da—

Oh, yeayea, Danny. Wit th' macaroons.

—Yeah, I have some samples here if yo—

Leave 'em here. Will taste em an letcha know. Come back inna cuppla days.

—OK, great. Well, so my name is Da—

Yeah, I goddit, Danny wit th' macaroons, Danny Macaroons, I goddit.

—Yeah so I'll come back in a few da—

Yea inna cuppla days, will letcha know.

—Ok, great, see you guys in a few da—

I laughed off the "Danny Macaroons" thing on my walk home, thinking it was just a funny Pleasant Avenue thing, like from *GoodFellas* or something.

A few days later I went back to the Love Café as promised. I opened the door and didn't get both feet in before Jay shouted, "DANNY MACAROOOOONS! Hey Pat, look, it's Danny Macaroons!"

And now, here we are.

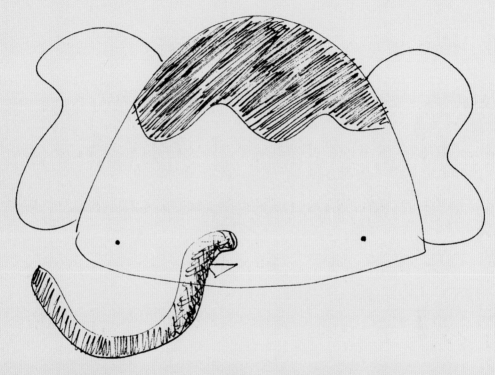

"Danny Macarooooons!
LOOK, IT'S DANNY MACAROONS!"

original vanilla macaroons

original VANILLA macaroons

It starts here, with the original vanilla-scented macaroon. It's the staple, the building block. Delicious and decadent all on its own, this cookie forms the basis of virtually every other one in this book. They're the simplest form and the one most commonly found at holidays and in stores. Perfect with coffee or tea, after dinner, or for a gluten-free breakfast treat.

Yield: Twenty-four 2-inch macaroons

MACAROONS:

- One 14-ounce can sweetened condensed milk
- 1 teaspoon vanilla extract
- One 14-ounce bag sweetened shredded coconut
- 2 large egg whites
- ¼ teaspoon kosher salt

1. Preheat the oven to 350°F with a rack in the center of the oven. Line a baking sheet with parchment.

2. In an extra-large bowl, measure out 10½ ounces by weight of the condensed milk and add the vanilla, incorporating it with a rubber spatula. If you don't have a scale, use approximately 8 ounces (1 cup) by liquid measure. Add the coconut to the condensed milk mixture and combine until thoroughly mixed.

3. Add the egg whites and salt to the bowl of a stand mixer (or small bowl if you're using a hand beater) and whip on medium-high until very stiff peaks form, 2½ to 3 minutes.

4. Using a rubber spatula, gently fold the whipped egg whites into the coconut mixture. After it's combined, push the mixture into one big blob to make it easier for you to portion out the macaroons.

5. Dip 2 spoons into a small bowl of water, shake them off, form the mixture into balls approximately 1½ inches in diameter, and place them on the baking sheet about 1 inch apart. (You can also form them by hand, but be sure to wet your fingers frequently.)

6. Place the sheet into the oven to bake for 20 to 25 minutes. After about 22 minutes, start checking for coloring. Look for an even, light golden color and for the undersides to be nicely tanned.

7. Remove from the oven and let the sheet rest on a cooling rack, leaving the macaroons on the sheet until they're cool enough for you to pull off (about 2 minutes depending on how sensitive your fingers are). Transfer the macaroons to the cooling rack to let cool completely. The macaroons will keep at room temperature for 3 to 5 days, for about 3 weeks in an airtight container in the fridge, and for a few months in the freezer.

CHOCOLATE *macaroons*

These are sneaky good, especially when still warm. The introduction of melted chocolate into the batter makes these bake up a little fudgier, a little denser, and just a little bit naughtier.

Yield: Twenty-four 2-inch macaroons

MACAROONS:

- 1½ ounces dark chocolate
- One 14-ounce can sweetened condensed milk
- ½ teaspoon vanilla extract
- One 14-ounce bag sweetened shredded coconut
- 2 large egg whites
- ¼ teaspoon kosher salt

1. Preheat the oven to 350°F with a rack in the center of the oven. Line a baking sheet with parchment.

2. Melt the dark chocolate in the microwave by placing in a microwave-safe bowl and microwaving on high in 30-second increments, stirring after each increment and until the chocolate is fully melted. (If you don't have a microwave, melt chocolate in a double boiler.)

3. In an extra-large bowl, measure out 10½ ounces by weight of the condensed milk. If you don't have a scale, use approximately 8 ounces (1 cup) by liquid measure. Add the melted chocolate and vanilla and incorporate with a rubber spatula. Add the coconut and combine until thoroughly mixed.

4. Add the egg whites and salt to the bowl of a stand mixer (or small bowl if you're using a hand beater) and whip on medium-high until very stiff peaks form, 2½ to 3 minutes.

5. Using a rubber spatula, gently fold the egg whites into the coconut mixture. After it's combined, push the mixture into one big blob to make it easier for you to portion out the macaroons.

6. Dip 2 spoons into a small bowl of water, shake them off, form the mixture into balls approximately 1½ inches in diameter, and place them on the baking sheet about 1 inch apart. (You can also form them by hand, but be sure to wet your fingers frequently.)

7. Place the sheet into the oven to bake for 20 to 25 minutes. After about 22 minutes, start checking for coloring. Look for an even, light golden color and for the undersides to be nicely tanned.

8. Remove from the oven and let the sheet rest on a cooling rack. Transfer the macaroons to a cooling rack to let cool completely. The macaroons will keep at room temperature for 3 to 5 days, for about 3 weeks in an airtight container in the fridge, and for a few months in the freezer.

chocolate macaroons

chocolate-dipped macaroons

CHOCOLATE-DIPPED *macaroons*

The first time I ever made macaroons, these were the ones I made. Sure, the original macaroon is the underpinning, but a luscious, dark chocolate with a strong character is such a perfect complement. Substitute milk chocolate (or white chocolate, but don't blame me if people don't eat the white chocolate ones) as you wish.

Yield: Twenty-four 2-inch macaroons

MACAROONS:

One 14-ounce can
    sweetened condensed milk
1 teaspoon vanilla extract
One 14-ounce bag
    sweetened shredded
    coconut
2 large egg whites
¼ teaspoon kosher salt
4 ounces chocolate of your
    choice, coarsely chopped
    into pieces the size of a
    quarter

1. Preheat the oven to 350°F with a rack in the center of the oven. Line a baking sheet with parchment.

2. In an extra-large bowl, measure out 10½ ounces by weight of the condensed milk. If you don't have a scale, use approximately 8 ounces (1 cup) by liquid measure. Add the vanilla and incorporate with a rubber spatula. Add the coconut and combine until thoroughly mixed.

3. Add the egg whites and salt to the bowl of a stand mixer (or small bowl if you're using a hand beater) and whip on medium-high until very stiff peaks form, 2½ to 3 minutes.

4. Using a rubber spatula, gently fold the egg whites into the coconut mixture. After it's combined, push the mixture into one big blob to make it easier for you to portion out the macaroons.

5. Dip 2 spoons into a small bowl of water, shake them off, form the mixture into balls approximately 1½ inches in diameter, and place them on the baking sheet about 1 inch apart. (You can also form them by hand, but be sure to wet your fingers frequently.)

6. Place the sheet into the oven to bake for 20 to 25 minutes. After about 22 minutes, start checking for coloring. Look for an even, light golden color and for the undersides to be nicely tanned.

7. Remove from the oven and let the sheet rest on a cooling rack, leaving the macaroons on the sheet until they're cool enough for you to pull off (about 2 minutes depending on how sensitive your fingers are). Transfer the macaroons to the cooling rack to let cool completely.

8. When the macaroons are cool, place the chocolate in a microwave-safe bowl and microwave on high for 1 minute. Stir thoroughly, then continue to microwave in 20-second increments until all the chocolate is melted and the chocolate feels quite warm (but not hot) when you touch it to your lip. (If you don't have a microwave, melt chocolate in a double boiler.) Then spoon or drizzle the chocolate on top of each of the macaroons. Alternatively, you can dip the tops of each macaroon into the chocolate. Or the bottoms. Or stick a skewer into each macaroon and completely cloak it. Knock yourself out.

9. Place back on the cooling rack and wait for the chocolate to set, or place the macaroons in the fridge for 15 to 30 minutes to greatly speed up the process.

10. The macaroons will keep uncovered for 3 to 5 days, for about 3 weeks in an airtight container in the fridge, and for a few months if stored in an airtight container in the freezer.

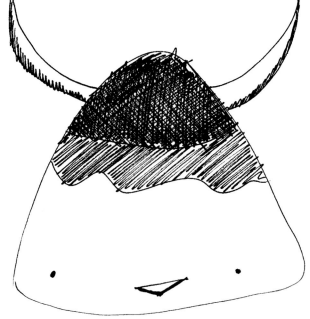

DOUBLE-CHOCOLATE *macaroons*

Studies show* that one out of every six people is a chocoholic. If you are a chocoholic, please, eat slowly.

Yield: Twenty-four 2-inch macaroons

MACAROONS:

5½ ounces dark chocolate
One 14-ounce can sweetened condensed milk
½ teaspoon vanilla extract
One 14-ounce bag sweetened shredded coconut
2 large egg whites
¼ teaspoon kosher salt

1. Preheat the oven to 350°F with a rack in the center of the oven. Line a baking sheet with parchment.

2. Melt 1½ ounces of the dark chocolate in the microwave by placing in a microwave-safe bowl and microwaving on high in 30-second increments, stirring after each increment and until the chocolate is fully melted.

3. In an extra-large bowl, measure out 10½ ounces by weight of the condensed milk. If you don't have a scale, use approximately 8 ounces (1 cup) by liquid measure. Add the melted chocolate and vanilla and incorporate with a rubber spatula. Add the coconut and combine until thoroughly mixed.

4. Add the egg whites and salt to the bowl of a stand mixer (or small bowl if you're using a hand beater) and whip on medium-high until very stiff peaks form, 2½ to 3 minutes.

5. Using a rubber spatula, gently fold the egg whites into the coconut mixture. After it's combined, push the mixture into one big blob to make it easier for you to portion out the macaroons.

6. Dip 2 spoons into a small bowl of water, shake them off, form the mixture into balls approximately 1½ inches in diameter, and place them on the baking sheet about 1 inch apart. (You can also form them by hand, but be sure to wet your fingers frequently.)

7. Place the sheet into the oven to bake for 20 to 25 minutes. After about 22 minutes, start checking for coloring. Look for an even, light golden color and for the undersides to be nicely tanned.

8. Remove from the oven and let the sheet rest on a cooling rack, leaving the macaroons on the sheet until they're cool enough for you to pull off (about 2 minutes depending on how sensitive your fingers are). Transfer the macaroons to the cooling rack to let cool completely.

*No they don't, at least not that I know of. But still, doesn't it seem like you know a few people who would consider themselves chocoholics? Everyone does. Maybe you're one of them!

double-chocolate macaroons

9. When the macaroons are cool, place the remaining 4 ounces chocolate in a microwave-safe bowl and microwave on high for 1 minute. Stir thoroughly, then continue to microwave in 20-second increments until all the chocolate is melted and the chocolate feels quite warm (but not hot) when you touch it to your lip. (If you don't have a microwave, melt chocolate in a double boiler.) Then spoon or drizzle the chocolate on top of each of the macaroons. Alternatively, you can dip the tops of each macaroon in chocolate. Or the bottoms. Or stick a skewer into each macaroon and completely cloak it. Knock yourself out.

10. Place back on the cooling rack and wait for the chocolate to set, or place the macaroons in the fridge for 15 to 30 minutes to greatly speed up the process.

11. The macaroons will keep uncovered for 3 to 5 days, for about 3 weeks in an airtight container in the fridge, and for a few months if stored in an airtight container in the freezer.

chocolate-almond macaroons

CHOCOLATE-ALMOND
macaroons

To paraphrase, there are times in a person's life when yo* feels like a nut. There are other times in a person's life when yo doesn't. These are for times when yo does.

Yield: Twenty-four 2-inch macaroons

MACAROONS:

- One 14-ounce can sweetened condensed milk
- 1 teaspoon vanilla extract
- One 14-ounce bag sweetened shredded coconut
- 2 large egg whites
- ¼ teaspoon kosher salt
- 24 whole almonds, plus ⅓ cup almonds, toasted (see Note below) and coarsely chopped
- 4 ounces chocolate of your choice, coarsely chopped into pieces the size of a quarter

1. Preheat the oven to 350°F with a rack in the center of the oven. Line a baking sheet with parchment.

2. In an extra-large bowl, measure out 10½ ounces by weight of the condensed milk. If you don't have a scale, use approximately 8 ounces (1 cup) by liquid measure. Add the vanilla and incorporate with a rubber spatula. Add the coconut and combine until thoroughly mixed.

3. Add the egg whites and salt to the bowl of a stand mixer (or small bowl if you're using a hand beater) and whip on medium-high until very stiff peaks form, 2½ to 3 minutes.

4. Using a rubber spatula, gently fold the egg whites into the coconut mixture. After it's combined, push the mixture into one big blob to make it easier for you to portion out the macaroons.

5. Dip 2 spoons into a small bowl of water, shake them off, form the mixture into balls approximately 1½ inches in diameter, and place them on the baking sheet about 1 inch apart. (You can also form them by hand, but be sure to wet your fingers frequently.)

6. When you've got the macaroons all out on the sheet, gently press a whole almond into the top of each macaroon. Place the sheet into the oven to bake for 20 to 25 minutes. After about 22 minutes, start checking for coloring. Look for an even, light golden color and for the undersides to be nicely tanned. The almonds will be a little bit darker but they should not be burnt.

---

*"Yo" is the gender-neutral pronoun that seemingly spontaneously appeared in Baltimore city schools in the early-to-mid 2000s. Elaine Stotko and Margaret Troyer, "A New Gender-Neutral Pronoun in Baltimore, Maryland: A Preliminary Study," *American Speech* 82, no. 3 (2007): 262–279.

7. Remove from the oven and let the sheet rest on a cooling rack, leaving the macaroons on the sheet until they're cool enough for you to pull off (about 2 minutes depending on how sensitive your fingers are). Transfer the macaroons to the cooling rack to let cool completely.

8. When the macaroons are cool, place the chocolate in a microwave-safe bowl and microwave on high for 1 minute. Stir thoroughly, then continue to microwave in 20-second increments until all the chocolate is melted and the chocolate feels quite warm (but not hot) when you touch it to your lip. (If you don't have a microwave, melt chocolate in a double boiler.) Then spoon or drizzle the chocolate on top of each of the macaroons. Alternatively, you can dip the tops or the sides of each macaroon in chocolate. Or the bottoms. Or stick a skewer into each macaroon and completely cloak it. Knock yourself out. Sprinkle with the chopped almonds.

9. Place back on the cooling sheet and wait for the chocolate to set, or place the macaroons in the fridge for 15 to 30 minutes to greatly speed up the process.

10. The macaroons will keep uncovered for 3 to 5 days, for about 3 weeks in an airtight container in the fridge, and for a few months if stored in an airtight container in the freezer.

note To toast the almonds, place them in a single layer on a baking sheet and place into a preheated 350°F oven for 25 minutes or until the almonds take on deeper coloring and become fragrant, giving them a shake and stir halfway through. Remove from the oven and set aside to cool.

"Sometimes

A CHOCOHOLIC FEELS LIKE A NUT."

double-chocolate & almond macaroons

DOUBLE-CHOCOLATE & ALMOND *macaroons*

Sometimes a chocoholic feels like a nut. . . .

Yield: Twenty-four 2-inch macaroons

MACAROONS:

- 5½ ounces dark chocolate
- One 14-ounce can sweetened condensed milk
- ½ teaspoon vanilla extract
- One 14-ounce bag sweetened shredded coconut
- 2 large egg whites
- ¼ teaspoon kosher salt
- 24 whole almonds, plus ⅓ cup almonds, toasted (see Note page 000) and coarsely chopped

1. Preheat the oven to 350°F with a rack in the center of the oven. Line a baking sheet with parchment.

2. Melt 1½ ounces of the dark chocolate in the microwave by placing in a microwave-safe bowl and microwaving on high in 30-second increments, stirring after each increment and until the chocolate is fully melted.

3. In an extra-large bowl, measure out 10½ ounces by weight of the condensed milk. If you don't have a scale, use approximately 8 ounces (1 cup) by liquid measure. Add the melted chocolate and vanilla and incorporate with a rubber spatula. Add the coconut and combine until thoroughly mixed.

4. Add the egg whites and salt to the bowl of a stand mixer (or small bowl if you're using a hand beater) and whip on medium-high until very stiff peaks form, 2½ to 3 minutes.

5. Using a rubber spatula, gently fold the egg whites into the coconut mixture. After it's combined, push the mixture into one big blob to make it easier for you to portion out the macaroons.

6. Dip 2 spoons into a small bowl of water, shake them off, form the mixture into balls approximately 1½ inches in diameter, and place them on the baking sheet about 1 inch apart. (You can also form them by hand, but be sure to wet your fingers frequently.)

7. When you've got the macaroons all out on the sheet, gently press a whole almond into the top of each macaroon. Place the sheet into the oven to bake for 20 to 25 minutes. After about 22 minutes, start checking for coloring. Look for an even, light golden color and for the undersides to be nicely tanned. The almonds will be a little bit darker but they should not be burnt.

8. Remove from the oven and let the sheet rest on a cooling rack, leaving the macaroons on the sheet until they're cool enough for you to pull off

(about 2 minutes depending on how sensitive your fingers are). Transfer the macaroons to the cooling rack to let cool completely.

9. When the macaroons are cool, place the remaining 4 ounces chocolate in a microwave-safe bowl and microwave on high for 1 minute. Stir thoroughly, then continue to microwave in 20-second increments until all the chocolate is melted and the chocolate feels quite warm (but not hot) when you touch it to your lip. (If you don't have a microwave, melt chocolate in a double boiler.) Then spoon or drizzle the chocolate on top of each of the macaroons. Alternatively, you can dip the tops of each macaroon in chocolate. Or the bottoms. Or stick a skewer into each macaroon and completely cloak it. Knock yourself out. Sprinkle with the chopped almonds.

10. Place back on the cooling rack and wait for the chocolate to set, or place the macaroons in the fridge for 15 to 30 minutes to greatly speed up the process.

11. The macaroons will keep uncovered for 3 to 5 days, for about 3 weeks in an airtight container in the fridge, and for a few months if stored in an airtight container in the freezer.

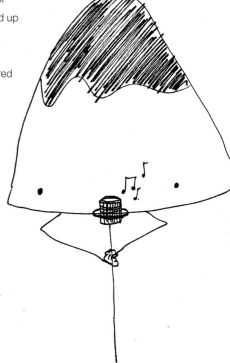

SALTED CARAMEL *macaroons*

This is the recipe that put Danny Macaroons on the map (and by "map" I mean convinced HMH to publish this book). I cannot guarantee that you will have similar success, but you may gain friends.

Yield: Twenty-four 2-inch macaroons

MACAROONS:

One 14-ounce can sweetened condensed milk
- 1 teaspoon vanilla extract
One 14-ounce bag sweetened shredded coconut
2 large egg whites
½ teaspoon kosher salt
¼ cup granulated sugar
1 tablespoon unsalted butter

1. Preheat the oven to 350°F with a rack in the center of the oven. Line a baking sheet with parchment.

2. In an extra-large bowl, measure out 10½ ounces by weight of the condensed milk. If you don't have a scale, use approximately 8 ounces (1 cup) by liquid measure. Add the vanilla and incorporate with a rubber spatula. Add the coconut and combine until thoroughly mixed.

3. Add the egg whites and ¼ teaspoon of the salt to the bowl of a stand mixer (or small bowl if you're using a hand beater) and whip on medium-high until very stiff peaks form, 2½ to 3 minutes.

4. Using a rubber spatula, gently fold the egg whites into the coconut mixture. After it's combined, push the mixture into one big blob to make it easier for you to portion out the macaroons.

5. Dip 2 spoons into a small bowl of water, shake them off, form the mixture into balls approximately 1½ inches in diameter, and place them on the baking sheet about 1 inch apart. (You can also form them by hand, but be sure to wet your fingers frequently.)

6. Place the sheet into the oven to bake for 20 to 25 minutes. After about 22 minutes, start checking for coloring. Look for an even, light golden color and for the undersides to be nicely tanned.

7. Remove from the oven and let the sheet rest on a cooling rack, leaving the macaroons on the sheet until they're cool enough for you to pull off (about 2 minutes depending on how sensitive your fingers are). Transfer the macaroons to the cooling rack to let cool completely.

8. While the macaroons are cooling, prepare the caramel. (WARNING: If you've never made caramel before, please be careful. Melted sugar is very hot and will burn you if you touch it or if it splashes on you.) Place the sugar in a small saucepan—the heavier the better—over medium heat and don't touch it until the sugar starts to melt. It'll slowly turn clear, then

salted caramel macaroons

pale yellow, and then start to darken. When it just starts to darken and/ or boil, start stirring carefully but rapidly to fully distribute any unmelted sugar throughout the pot. Keep stirring until all the sugar is melted and there are no lumps, then turn the heat down to low and when the sugar has a nice copper color to it, add the butter. Stir to mix the sugar and butter together, then add the remaining ¼ teaspoon salt and continue stirring until the butter is completely integrated with the sugar. If it starts to smoke, remove the pot from the heat. When the caramel has a nice caramel color to it, remove from the heat and, using a small spoon, drizzle on top of the macaroons.

9. The macaroons will keep uncovered for 3 to 5 days, for about 3 weeks in an airtight container in the fridge, and for a few months if stored in an airtight container in the freezer.

CHOCOLATE–SALTED CARAMEL *macaroons*

There's an ongoing debate between my mother and everyone else about whether or not these are better than the original Salted Caramel Macaroons. She loves these very dearly, and I'm tempted to say "Who can argue with a mother?" but I also make macaroons for a living, so what do I know?

Yield: Twenty-four 2-inch macaroons

MACAROONS:

- 1½ ounces dark chocolate
- One 14-ounce can sweetened condensed milk
- ½ teaspoon vanilla extract
- One 14-ounce bag sweetened shredded coconut
- 2 large egg whites
- ½ teaspoon kosher salt
- Heaping ¼ cup granulated sugar
- 1 tablespoon unsalted butter

1. Preheat the oven to 350°F with a rack in the center of the oven. Line a baking sheet with parchment.

2. Melt the dark chocolate in the microwave by placing in a microwave-safe bowl and microwaving on high in 30-second increments, stirring after each increment and until the chocolate is fully melted. (If you don't have a microwave, melt chocolate in a double boiler.)

3. In an extra-large bowl, measure out 10½ ounces by weight of the condensed milk. If you don't have a scale, use approximately 8 ounces (1 cup) by liquid measure. Add the melted chocolate and vanilla and incorporate with a rubber spatula. Add the coconut and combine until thoroughly mixed.

4. Add the egg whites and ¼ teaspoon of the salt to the bowl of a stand mixer (or small bowl if you're using a hand beater) and whip on medium-high until very stiff peaks form, 2½ to 3 minutes.

5. Using a rubber spatula, gently fold the egg whites into the coconut mixture. After it's combined, push the mixture into one big blob to make it easier for you to portion out the macaroons.

6. Dip 2 spoons into a small bowl of water, shake them off, form the mixture into balls approximately 1½ inches in diameter, and place them on the baking sheet about 1 inch apart. (You can also form them by hand, but be sure to wet your fingers frequently.)

7. Place the sheet into the oven to bake for 20 to 25 minutes. After about 22 minutes, start checking for coloring. Look for an even, light golden color and for the undersides to be nicely tanned.

8. Remove from the oven and let the sheet rest on a cooling rack, leaving the macaroons on the sheet until they're cool enough for you to pull off

chocolate-salted caramel macaroons

(about 2 minutes depending on how sensitive your fingers are). Transfer the macaroons to the cooling rack to let cool completely.

9. While the macaroons are cooling, prepare the caramel. (WARNING: If you've never made caramel before, please be careful. Melted sugar is very hot and will burn you if you touch it or if it splashes on you.) Place the sugar in a small saucepan—the heavier the better—over medium heat and don't touch it until the sugar starts to melt. It'll slowly turn clear, then pale yellow, and then start to darken. When it just starts to darken and/or boil, start stirring carefully but rapidly to fully distribute any unmelted sugar throughout the pot. Keep stirring until all the sugar is melted and there are no lumps, then turn the heat down to low and when the sugar has a nice copper color to it, add the butter. Stir to mix the sugar and butter together, then add the remaining ¼ teaspoon salt and continue stirring until the butter is completely integrated with the sugar. If it starts to smoke, remove the pot from the heat. When the caramel has a nice caramel color to it, remove from the heat and, using a small spoon, drizzle on top of the macaroons.

10. The macaroons will keep uncovered for 3 to 5 days, for about 3 weeks in an airtight container in the fridge, and for a few months if stored in an airtight container in the freezer.

AMARETTO *macaroons* (OR TRIPLE-ALMOND *macaroons*)

The delightful combination of coconut and almond has already been documented in this book, but the combination is so good that I wanted to take it further. This recipe is much less about the amaretto than it is about the different forms of almond working together to create a flavor that is so delicately delicious you'll want to make these over and over again. Please note: I hate almond extract (and almond paste) and will never use it. If you like it, though, feel free to replace the vanilla with almond extract and call these Quadruple-Almond Macaroons.

Yield: Twenty-four 2-inch macaroons

MACAROONS:

One 14-ounce can sweetened condensed milk
2 tablespoons almond butter
5 teaspoons amaretto
½ cup almonds, toasted (see Note page 000) and pretty finely chopped
½ teaspoon vanilla extract
One 14-ounce bag sweetened shredded coconut
2 large egg whites
¼ teaspoon kosher salt

1. Preheat the oven to 350°F with a rack in the center of the oven. Line a baking sheet with parchment.

2. In an extra-large bowl, measure out 8 ounces of the condensed milk by weight. If you don't have a scale, use just over half of the can. Add the almond butter, amaretto, ¼ cup of the almonds, and the vanilla and incorporate with a rubber spatula. Add the coconut and combine until thoroughly mixed.

3. Add the egg whites and salt to the bowl of a stand mixer (or small bowl if you're using a hand beater) and whip on medium-high until very stiff peaks form, 2½ to 3 minutes.

4. Using a rubber spatula, gently fold the egg whites into the coconut mixture. After it's combined, push the mixture into one big blob to make it easier for you to portion out the macaroons.

5. Dip 2 spoons into a small bowl of water, shake them off, form the mixture into balls approximately 1½ inches in diameter, and place them on the baking sheet about 1 inch apart. (You can also form them by hand, but be sure to wet your fingers frequently.)

6. When you've got the macaroons all out on the sheet, sprinkle the remaining ¼ cup chopped almonds onto each macaroon, pressing them in lightly. Place the sheet into the oven to bake for 20 to 25 minutes. After about 22 minutes, start checking for coloring. Look for an even, light golden color and for the undersides to be nicely tanned.

amaretto macaroons (or triple almond macaroons)

7. Remove from the oven and let the sheet rest on a cooling rack, leaving the macaroons on the sheet until they're cool enough for you to pull off (about 2 minutes depending on how sensitive your fingers are). Transfer the macaroons to the cooling rack to let cool completely. The macaroons will keep at room temperature for 3 to 5 days, for about 3 weeks in an airtight container in the fridge, and for a few months if stored in an airtight container in the freezer.

OIRISH (BAILEYS) *mc'roons*

I have a friend and her name is Grace. She said a lot of nice things about the macaroons, but one negative thing: that I had no Baileys Irish Cream in my macaroons. Well, Grace, consider that wrong righted.

Yield: Twenty-four 2-inch macaroons

MACAROONS:

- One 14-ounce can sweetened condensed milk
- 2 tablespoons Baileys Irish Cream
- ¼ teaspoon vanilla extract
- One 14-ounce bag sweetened shredded coconut
- 2 large egg whites
- ¼ teaspoon kosher salt
- Green sugar crystals, for sprinkling

1. Preheat the oven to 350°F with a rack in the center of the oven. Line a baking sheet with parchment.

2. In an extra-large bowl, measure out 10½ ounces by weight of the condensed milk. If you don't have a scale, use approximately 8 ounces (1 cup) by liquid measure. Add the Baileys and vanilla and incorporate with a rubber spatula. Add the coconut and combine until thoroughly mixed.

3. Add the egg whites and salt to the bowl of a stand mixer (or small bowl if you're using a hand beater) and whip on medium-high until very stiff peaks form, 2½ to 3 minutes.

4. Using a rubber spatula, gently fold the egg whites into the coconut mixture. After it's combined, push the mixture into one big blob to make it easier for you to portion out the macaroons.

5. Dip 2 spoons into a small bowl of water, shake them off, form the mixture into balls approximately 1½ inches in diameter, and place them on the baking sheet about 1 inch apart. (You can also form them by hand, but be sure to wet your fingers frequently.)

6. Sprinkle green sugar crystals over each macaroon. Place the sheet into the oven to bake for 19 minutes. After about 17 minutes, start checking for coloring. Look for an even, light golden color and for the undersides to be nicely tanned. These macaroons will darken a bit more quickly than normal, so keep a close eye on them.

7. Remove from the oven and transfer the macaroons to a cooling rack to let cool completely. The macaroons will keep at room temperature for 3 to 5 days, for about 3 weeks in an airtight container in the fridge, and for a few months if stored in an airtight container in the freezer.

oirish (baileys) mcroons

bourbon macaroons

BOURBON *macaroons*

Grace* got me thinking about what other alcohols could work in macaroons. I thought about what I like to drink (tequila, rum, whiskey), and about what had enough character to stand up to the mighty coconut, and decided that bourbon was the answer. Use whichever you like—I think Maker's Mark is nice.

Yield: Twenty-four 2-inch macaroons

MACAROONS:

One 14-ounce can
sweetened condensed milk
2 tablespoons Maker's Mark
or your favorite bourbon
(plus 2 tablespoons
bourbon reduction; see
Note below)
1 whole nutmeg (optional)
One 14-ounce bag
sweetened shredded
coconut
2 large egg whites
¼ teaspoon kosher salt

1. Preheat the oven to 350°F with a rack in the center of the oven. Line a baking sheet with parchment.

2. In an extra-large bowl, measure out 10½ ounces by weight of the condensed milk. If you don't have a scale, use approximately 8 ounces (1 cup) by liquid measure. Add the Maker's Mark (and reduction, if desired) and about 15 passes of the nutmeg over a nutmeg grater, if desired, and incorporate with a rubber spatula. Add the coconut and combine until thoroughly mixed.

3. Add the egg whites and salt to the bowl of a stand mixer (or small bowl if you're using a hand beater) and whip on medium-high until very stiff peaks form, 2½ to 3 minutes.

4. Using a rubber spatula, gently fold the egg whites into the coconut mixture. After it's combined, push the mixture into one big blob to make it easier for you to portion out the macaroons.

5. Dip 2 spoons into a small bowl of water, shake them off, form the mixture into balls approximately 1½ inches in diameter, and place them on the baking sheet about 1 inch apart. (You can also form them by hand, but be sure to wet your fingers frequently.)

6. Place the sheet into the oven to bake for 20 to 25 minutes. After about 21 minutes, start checking for coloring. Look for an even, light golden color and for the undersides to be nicely tanned. These macaroons will darken a bit more quickly than normal, so keep a close eye on them starting at about 19 minutes.

7. Remove from the oven and let the sheet rest on a cooling rack, leaving the macaroons on the sheet until they're cool enough for you to pull off

*See Oirish Mc'roons (page 54).

(about 2 minutes depending on how sensitive your fingers are). Transfer the macaroons to the cooling rack to let cool completely. The macaroons will keep at room temperature for 3 to 5 days, for about 3 weeks in an airtight container in the fridge, and for a few months if stored in an airtight container in the freezer.

note The bourbon reduction is totally optional and it really only makes sense if you've got 12 ounces (1½ cups) of bourbon to spare. If you do, just simmer the 12 ounces of bourbon down to about 2 ounces and reserve.

"Use whatever you like— I THINK MAKER'S Mark IS NICE."

eggnog macaroons

EGGNOG *macaroons*

There's pretty much nothing that can't be reinvented or reimagined. Eggnog is no different. And since macaroons are a Christmas tradition for some, why not combine the two and see how crazy we can get? In reality, macaroons provide the perfect vehicle for classic eggnog ingredients: nutmeg and bourbon.

Yield: Twenty-four 2-inch macaroons

MACAROONS:

One 14-ounce can
sweetened condensed milk
2 tablespoons Maker's Mark
or your favorite bourbon
¼ teaspoon vanilla extract
¼ teaspoon ground nutmeg
Pinch of ground cinnamon
One 14-ounce bag
sweetened shredded
coconut
2 large egg whites
¼ teaspoon kosher salt
1 whole nutmeg

1. Preheat the oven to 350°F with a rack in the center of the oven. Line a baking sheet with parchment.

2. In an extra-large bowl, measure out 10½ ounces by weight of the condensed milk. If you don't have a scale, use approximately 8 ounces (1 cup) by liquid measure. Add the Maker's Mark, vanilla, ground nutmeg, and cinnamon and incorporate with a rubber spatula. Add the coconut and combine until thoroughly mixed.

3. Add the egg whites and salt to the bowl of a stand mixer (or small bowl if you're using a hand beater) and whip on medium-high until very stiff peaks form, 2½ to 3 minutes.

4. Using a rubber spatula, gently fold the egg whites into the coconut mixture. After it's combined, push the mixture into one big blob to make it easier for you to portion out the macaroons.

5. Dip 2 spoons into a small bowl of water, shake them off, form the mixture into balls approximately 1½ inches in diameter, and place them on the baking sheet about 1 inch apart. (You can also form them by hand, but be sure to wet your fingers frequently.)

6. Place the sheet into the oven to bake for 24 minutes. After about 19 minutes, start checking for coloring. Look for an even, light golden color and for the undersides to be nicely tanned. These macaroons will darken a bit more quickly than normal, so keep a close eye on them.

7. Remove from the oven and transfer the macaroons to a cooling rack to let cool completely.

8. Garnish with a few passes of freshly grated nutmeg before serving. The macaroons will keep at room temperature for 3 to 5 days, for about 3 weeks in an airtight container in the fridge, and for a few months if stored in an airtight container in the freezer.

CHOCOLATE-STOUT *macaroons*

This has become one of my favorite macaroon recipes. I had the idea for it while I was in Hawaii drinking a CoCoNut PorTeR from the Maui Brewing Company. It was such a great beer with so much complexity that I thought a macaroon based on it would be fantastic. And it is. I absolutely love how the bitterness of the stout balances some of the macaroon's sweetness and how the chocolate rounds out the party.

Yield: Twenty-four 2-inch macaroons

MACAROONS:

One 14-ounce can sweetened condensed milk
One 12-ounce or 16-ounce bottle of your favorite stout (mine is Brooklyn Brewery's Black Chocolate Stout, but if you don't have a favorite, Guinness will do), reduced to about 2 ounces (see Note page 64)
½ teaspoon vanilla extract
½ ounce of chocolate, melted
One 14-ounce bag sweetened shredded coconut
2 large egg whites
¼ teaspoon kosher salt

1. Preheat the oven to 350°F with a rack in the center of the oven. Line a baking sheet with parchment.

2. In an extra-large bowl, measure out 10½ ounces by weight of the condensed milk. If you don't have a scale, use approximately 8 ounces (1 cup) by liquid measure. Add the stout, vanilla, and melted chocolate and incorporate with a rubber spatula. Add the coconut to the condensed milk mixture and combine until thoroughly mixed.

3. Add the egg whites and salt to the bowl of a stand mixer (or small bowl if you're using a hand beater) and whip on medium-high until very stiff peaks form, 2½ to 3 minutes.

4. Using a rubber spatula, gently fold the egg whites into the coconut mixture. After it's combined, push the mixture into one big blob to make it easier for you to portion out the macaroons.

5. Dip 2 spoons into a small bowl of water, shake them off, form the mixture into balls approximately 1½ inches in diameter, and place them on the baking sheet about 1 inch apart. (You can also form them by hand, but be sure to wet your fingers frequently.)

6. Place the sheet into the oven to bake for 20 to 25 minutes. After about 22 minutes, start checking for coloring. Look for an even, light golden color and for the undersides to be nicely tanned.

7. Remove from the oven and let the sheet rest on a cooling rack, leaving the macaroons on the sheet until they're cool enough for you to pull off (about 2 minutes depending on how sensitive your fingers are). Transfer the macaroons to the cooling rack to let cool completely. The macaroons will keep at room temperature for 3 to 5 days, for about 3 weeks in an

chocolate-stout macaroons

airtight container in the fridge, and for a few months if stored in an airtight container in the freezer.

note To reduce the beer, pour into a heavy saucepan and boil until it reduces to 2 to 4 tablespoons. Your goal is to create a syrup from the stout. Be careful at the beginning that the beer doesn't foam over the pot, and keep reducing it until when you tilt the pot, the reduction coats the bottom or when you dip a spoon into it, the beer clings to the spoon like a thin maple syrup. It should be bubbling way more like a tar pit than a pot of liquid by the time you're finished with it.

PIÑA COLADA *macaroons*

I know that piña coladas are delicious. I don't even need to taste them to know it. When I do taste them, my feelings are confirmed. So why don't I drink them all the time? I have no idea. Similarly, I make these so infrequently—and each time I make them, I ask myself why I don't make them more often. Coconut and pineapple are such wonderful friends, and I'm asking you to make these more often. Everyone will be happier that way.

Yield: Twenty-four 2-inch macaroons

MACAROONS:

    One 14-ounce can sweetened condensed milk

2¼ ounces unsweetened, dried, unsulfured pineapple (½ cup chopped)

2 tablespoons rum (optional)

¼ teaspoon vanilla extract

    One 14-ounce bag sweetened shredded coconut

2 large egg whites

¼ teaspoon kosher salt

1. Preheat the oven to 350°F with a rack in the center of the oven. Line a baking sheet with parchment.

2. Add 10½ ounces by weight of the condensed milk to a blender. If you don't have a scale, use approximately 8 ounces (1 cup) by liquid measure. Add the pineapple, rum (if desired), and vanilla to the blender and blend until smooth-ish; it may still have some pineapple chunks and that's OK. Pour into an extra-large bowl, add the coconut, and combine until thoroughly mixed.

3. Add the egg whites and salt to the bowl of a stand mixer (or small bowl if you're using a hand beater) and whip on medium-high until very stiff peaks form, 2½ to 3 minutes.

4. Using a rubber spatula, gently fold the egg whites into the coconut mixture. After it's combined, push the mixture into one big blob to make it easier for you to portion out the macaroons.

5. Dip 2 spoons into a small bowl of water, shake them off, form the mixture into balls approximately 1½ inches in diameter, and place them on the baking sheet about 1 inch apart. (You can also form them by hand, but be sure to wet your fingers frequently.)

6. Place the sheet into the oven to bake for 20 minutes. After about 18 minutes, start checking for coloring. Look for an even, light golden color and for the undersides to be nicely tanned.

7. Remove from the oven and let the sheet rest on a cooling rack, leaving the macaroons on the sheet until they're cool enough for you to pull off (about 2 minutes depending on how sensitive your fingers are). Transfer the macaroons to the cooling rack to let cool completely. The macaroons will keep at room temperature for 3 to 5 days, for about 3 weeks in an airtight container in the fridge, and for a few months if stored in an airtight container in the freezer.

piña colada macaroons

tiramisu macaroons

TIRAMISU *macaroons*

Something spoke to me: I had visions of Marsala and mascarpone swimming through my mind. Something else happened and I had an idea for tiramisu macaroons two ways: as a mounded macaroon and as a sandwich. I think I prefer the sandwiches a little bit more, but they're both delicious. Serve either version dusted with some cocoa powder.

Yield: Twenty-four 2-inch macaroons or twelve 2½-inch macaroon sandwiches

MACAROONS:

    One 14-ounce can sweetened condensed milk

2 ounces mascarpone cheese

2 tablespoons freshly brewed espresso, cooled (can also use very strong coffee)

1 tablespoon Marsala

½ teaspoon vanilla extract

½ teaspoon ground cinnamon

½ teaspoon unsweetened cocoa powder, plus extra for dusting (optional)

    One 14-ounce bag sweetened shredded coconut

2 large egg whites

¼ teaspoon kosher salt

For tiramisu sandwiches with Marsala-mascarpone shells and chocolate-espresso ganache filling:

6 ounces dark chocolate, chopped into pieces roughly the size of a nickel or smaller ½ cup heavy cream

1. Preheat the oven to 350°F with a rack in the center of the oven. Line a baking sheet with parchment (2 baking sheets if you're making the sandwiches).

If you're making the macaroons:

2. In a large bowl, measure out 7 ounces by weight of the condensed milk. If you don't have a scale, use approximately 5⅓ ounces (⅔ cup) by liquid measure. Add the mascarpone, espresso, Marsala, vanilla, cinnamon, and cocoa powder and combine thoroughly. Add the coconut and combine until thoroughly mixed.

If you're making the sandwiches:

2. Add 7 ounces of the condensed milk, the mascarpone, Marsala, and vanilla to a large bowl and stir well to combine (reserve the espresso and cinnamon for the ganache and omit the cocoa powder). Add the coconut and combine until thoroughly mixed.

For both:

3. Add the egg whites and salt to the bowl of a stand mixer (or small bowl if you're using a hand beater) and whip on medium-high until very stiff peaks form, 2½ to 3 minutes.

4. Using a rubber spatula, gently fold the egg whites into the coconut mixture. After it's combined, push the mixture into one big blob to make it easier for you to portion out the macaroons.

5. Dip 2 spoons into a small bowl of water, shake them off, form the mixture into balls approximately 1½ inches in diameter, and place them on the baking sheet about 1 inch apart (if you're making the sandwiches, form the mixture into balls ¼ inch in diameter and then flatten out into a disk on the baking sheets).

6. Place the sheet into the oven to bake for 20 to 25 minutes. After about 22 minutes, start checking for coloring. Look for an even, light golden color and for the undersides to be nicely tanned. (If you're making sandwiches, bake for 10 to 15 minutes, or until the edges are just golden brown.)

7. Remove from the oven and let the sheet rest on a cooling rack, leaving the macaroons on the sheet until they're cool enough for you to pull off (about 2 minutes depending on how sensitive your fingers are). Transfer the macaroons to the cooling rack to let cool completely. Dust the macaroons with cocoa powder, if desired. The macaroons will keep at room temperature for 3 to 5 days, for about 3 weeks in an airtight container in the fridge, and for a few months if stored in an airtight container in the freezer.

If you're making sandwiches, follow these instructions for the chocolate-espresso ganache and assembly:

8. Place the chocolate into a large bowl.

9. Heat the cream over medium heat until very hot but not boiling. Add the espresso and cinnamon. Pour the cream over the chocolate and whisk until smooth and thick, about 3 minutes.

10. Let cool, and then spread over the flat side of one shell and attach another shell, flat side in, to make your sandwich. Repeat. Refrigerate for 15 to 30 minutes to set.

"Something spoke to me:
I HAD VISIONS OF

MARSALA
— AND —
Mascarpone
SWIMMING THROUGH MY MIND."

amaro macaroons

AMARO *macaroons*

These might be a little confusing at first, given the existence of amaretti, the Italian macaroon. However, there are no almonds in this recipe, just amaro, the sweet Italian nectar of digestion.

Yield: Twenty-four 2-inch macaroons

MACAROONS:

- 2 cups amaro (Averna, Fernet, etc.)
- One 14-ounce can sweetened condensed milk
- ⅛ teaspoon vanilla extract
- ⅛ teaspoon grated grapefruit zest
- ⅛ teaspoon grated lemon zest
- One 14-ounce bag sweetened shredded coconut
- 2 large egg whites
- ¼ teaspoon kosher salt

1. Add the amaro to a small saucepan and simmer over medium-high heat until about ¼ cup remains. Remove from the heat and set aside.

2. Preheat the oven to 350°F with a rack in the center of the oven. Line a baking sheet with parchment.

3. In an extra-large bowl, measure out 8 ounces of the condensed milk. If you don't have a scale, use just over half of the can. Add the amaro reduction, vanilla, and both zests and incorporate with a rubber spatula. Add the coconut to the condensed milk mixture and combine until thoroughly mixed.

4. Add the egg whites and salt to the bowl of a stand mixer (or small bowl if you're using a hand beater) and whip on medium-high until very stiff peaks form, 2½ to 3 minutes.

5. Using a rubber spatula, gently fold the whipped egg whites into the coconut mixture. After it's combined, push the mixture into one big blob to make it easier for you to portion out the macaroons.

6. Dip 2 spoons into a small bowl of water, shake them off, form the mixture into balls approximately 1½ inches in diameter, and place them on the baking sheet about 1 inch apart. (You can also form them by hand, but be sure to wet your fingers frequently.)

7. Place the sheet into the oven to bake for 20 to 25 minutes. After about 22 minutes, start checking for coloring. Look for an even, light golden color and for the undersides to be nicely tanned.

8. Remove from the oven and let rest on a cooling rack, leaving the macaroons on the sheet until they're cool enough for you to pull off (about 2 minutes depending on how sensitive your fingers are). Transfer the macaroons to the cooling rack to let cool completely. The macaroons will keep at room temperature for 3 to 5 days, for about 3 weeks in an airtight container in the fridge, and for a few months if stored in the freezer.

red velvet macaroons

RED VELVET *macaroons*

I'll confess: I have no idea what red velvet cake is or why it exists. I've read plenty about the chemical reactions that turn batter purpley red but I still don't get why we make it. What I do get, though, is that people LOVE red velvet. If you want to wow a crowd, just whip up a batch of these, put them out, and stand back and watch. And really, why wouldn't people be wowed? The color contrast is striking; the textural contrast—between the crisp exterior, soft interior, smooth frosting, and toasted pecans—is something that's almost impossible to achieve with cake; and the novelty factor is high. And they're delicious, too.

Yield: Twenty-four 2-inch macaroons

MACAROONS:

    One 14-ounce can of
      sweetened condensed milk
2   teaspoons unsweetened
      cocoa powder
¾   teaspoon red food coloring
¼   teaspoon vanilla extract
2   drops of blue food coloring
2   large egg whites
¼   teaspoon kosher salt
    One 14-ounce bag
      sweetened shredded
      coconut

1. Preheat the oven to 350°F with a rack in the center of the oven. Line a baking sheet with parchment.

2. In an extra-large bowl, measure out 10½ ounces by weight of the condensed milk. If you don't have a scale, use approximately 8 ounces (1 cup) by liquid measure. Add the cocoa powder, ¼ teaspoon of the red food coloring, the vanilla, and blue food coloring and mix with a rubber spatula until fully incorporated.

3. Add the egg whites and salt to the bowl of a stand mixer (or small bowl if you're using a hand beater) and whip on medium-high until very stiff peaks form, 2½ to 3 minutes.

4. Empty the coconut into a gallon-size zip-top bag and add the remaining ½ teaspoon red food coloring. Seal the bag and shake vigorously until the color is fully absorbed by the coconut, then add the coconut to the condensed milk mixture and mix until fully combined. Gently fold the whipped egg whites into the coconut mixture. After it's combined, push the mixture into one big blob to make it easier for you to portion out the macaroons.

5. Dip 2 spoons into a small bowl of water, shake them off, form the mixture into balls approximately 1½ inches in diameter, and place them on the baking sheet about 1 inch apart. (You can also form them by hand, but be sure to wet your fingers frequently.)

6. Place the sheet into the oven to bake for 20 to 25 minutes. After about

CREAM CHEESE FROSTING AND TOPPING:

- 8 ounces cream cheese, at room temperature
- 4 tablespoons (½ stick) unsalted butter, at room temperature
- ½ teaspoon vanilla extract
- 1 cup confectioners' sugar, sifted
- 1 cup pecans, toasted (see Note below) and coarsely chopped

22 minutes, start checking for coloring. Look for an even, light golden color and for the undersides to be nicely tanned.

7. Remove from the oven and let the sheet rest on a cooling rack, leaving the macaroons on the sheet until they're cool enough for you to pull off (about 2 minutes depending on how sensitive your fingers are). Transfer the macaroons to the cooling rack to let cool completely.

8. While the macaroons are cooling, prepare your frosting. In the bowl of a stand mixer fitted with the paddle attachment (or in a small bowl if using a hand mixer), beat together the cream cheese and butter until smooth, scraping down the sides of the bowl if the mixture creeps up or sticks. Add the vanilla and then, gradually and on low speed, the confectioners' sugar until fully incorporated. Feel free to taste the mixture along the way and adjust the sugar until it's as sweet as you'd like. Then increase the speed to medium-high and mix until light and fluffy, about 1 minute.

9. When the macaroons are cool, add the topping to each one using a butter knife or, if you have one, an icing or frosting spatula. After the macaroons are frosted, sprinkle the pecans on top—you may have to push the pecans into the icing. If you're going to store these, it's best to keep the frosting stored separately in an airtight container in the fridge and frost your macaroons when you want to eat them. The icing will keep in the refrigerator for at least 1 week. Store the macaroons in an airtight container in the fridge for about 3 weeks.

note To toast the pecans, place the pecans in a single layer on a baking sheet and place into a preheated 300°F oven for 25 minutes or until the pecans take on deeper coloring and are somewhat fragrant, giving them a shake and a stir halfway through. Remove from the oven and set aside to cool.

ROCKY ROAD *macaroons*

Another classically American dessert combination reimagined in macaroon form. You might want to make two batches and keep one hidden just for you.

Yield: Twenty-four 2-inch macaroons

MACAROONS:
- One 14-ounce can sweetened condensed milk
- 1 teaspoon vanilla extract
- One 14-ounce bag sweetened shredded coconut
- 2 large egg whites
- ¼ teaspoon kosher salt
- One 10.5-ounce (or smaller) package mini marshmallows
- 1 cup walnuts, toasted (see Note below), half chopped coarsely, half left whole (you'll need 24 whole ones)
- 4 ounces chocolate of your choice, coarsely chopped into pieces the size of a quarter

1. Preheat the oven to 350°F with a rack in the center of the oven. Line a baking sheet with parchment.

2. In an extra-large bowl, measure out 10½ ounces by weight of the condensed milk. If you don't have a scale, use approximately 8 ounces (1 cup) by liquid measure. Add the vanilla and incorporate with a rubber spatula. Add the coconut to the condensed milk mixture and combine until thoroughly mixed.

3. Add the egg whites and salt to the bowl of a stand mixer (or small bowl if you're using a hand beater) and whip on medium-high until very stiff peaks form, 2½ to 3 minutes.

4. Using a rubber spatula, gently fold the egg whites into the coconut mixture. After it's combined, push the mixture into one big blob to make it easier for you to portion out the macaroons.

5. Dip 2 spoons into a small bowl of water, shake them off, form the mixture into balls approximately 1½ inches in diameter, and place them on the baking sheet about 1 inch apart. (You can also form them by hand, but be sure to wet your fingers frequently.)

6. Push 2 mini marshmallows into the center of each macaroon and fold up the sides of each macaroon to fully enclose the marshmallow. Lightly press a whole walnut into the top of each newly formed macaroon ball.

7. Place the sheet into the oven to bake for 20 to 25 minutes. After about 22 minutes, start checking for coloring. Look for an even, light golden color and for the undersides to be nicely tanned.

8. Remove from the oven and let the sheet rest on a cooling rack, leaving the macaroons on the sheet until they're cool enough for you to pull off (about 2 minutes depending on how sensitive your fingers are). Transfer the macaroons to the cooling rack to let cool completely.

9. When the macaroons are cool, place the chocolate in a microwave-

rocky road macaroons

safe bowl and microwave on high for 1 minute. Stir thoroughly, then continue to microwave in 20-second increments until all the chocolate is melted and the chocolate feels quite warm (but not hot) when you touch it to your lip. (If you don't have a microwave, melt chocolate in a double boiler.) Then spoon or drizzle the chocolate on top of each of the macaroons. Alternatively, you can dip the tops of each macaroon in chocolate. Or the bottoms. Or stick a skewer into each macaroon and completely cloak it. Knock yourself out. Sprinkle with the chopped walnuts.

10. Place back on the cooling rack and wait for the chocolate to set, or place the macaroons in the fridge for 15 to 30 minutes to greatly speed up the process.

11. The macaroons will keep uncovered for 3 to 5 days, for about 3 weeks in an airtight container in the fridge, and for a few months if stored in an airtight container in the freezer.

note To toast the walnuts, place the walnuts in a single layer on a baking sheet and place into a preheated 300°F oven for 20 minutes or until the walnuts take on deeper coloring and are somewhat fragrant, giving them a shake and a stir halfway through. Remove from the oven and set aside to cool.

note As an alternative, you can make these as sandwiches by spreading ganache on one half and marshmallow on the other, pressing chopped toasted walnuts into the ganache (or marshmallow), and then pressing the two halves together.

"Sometimes
YOU HAVE TO GIVE A LITTLE."

STOOPID *macaroons*

I credit Christina Tosi of Momofuku Milk Bar for these. Her compost cookies are wildly popular and they're filled with all kinds of junk. I'm a purist at heart, I prefer fewer ingredients in my food, and so her compost cookies kind of piss me off. But you know what? They're delicious. And so are these. Sometimes you have to give a little, you know?

Yield: Twenty-four 2-inch macaroons

MACAROONS:

One 14-ounce can sweetened condensed milk

½ teaspoon vanilla extract

One 14-ounce bag sweetened shredded coconut

2 ounces thin, salted pretzels, crunched up into small pieces (but not ground up)

2 ounces potato chips (I find ridged work better, but as you like), coarsely crunched up

1 Butterfinger bar, half chopped up, the other half reserved for Halloween

2 large egg whites

¼ teaspoon kosher salt

Optional:

2 ounces dark chocolate, coarsely chopped into pieces the size of a quarter

1. Preheat the oven to 350°F with a rack in the center of the oven. Line a baking sheet with parchment.

2. In an extra-large bowl, measure out 10½ ounces by weight of the condensed milk. If you don't have a scale, use approximately 8 ounces (1 cup) by liquid measure. Add the vanilla, 10 ounces of the coconut, the pretzels, potato chips, and Butterfinger and combine with a rubber spatula until thoroughly mixed.

3. Add the egg whites and salt to the bowl of a stand mixer (or small bowl if you're using a hand beater) and whip on medium-high until very stiff peaks form, 2½ to 3 minutes.

4. Using a rubber spatula, gently fold the egg whites into the coconut mixture. After it's combined, push the mixture into one big blob to make it easier for you to portion out the macaroons.

5. Dip 2 spoons into a small bowl of water, shake them off, form the mixture into balls approximately 1½ inches in diameter, and place them on the baking sheet about 1 inch apart. (You can also form them by hand, but be sure to wet your fingers frequently.)

6. Place the sheet into the oven to bake for 20 to 25 minutes. After about 22 minutes, start checking for coloring. Look for an even, light golden color and for the undersides to be nicely tanned.

7. Remove from the oven and let the sheet rest on a cooling rack, leaving the macaroons on the sheet until they're cool enough for you to pull off (about 2 minutes depending on how sensitive your fingers are). Transfer the macaroons to the cooling rack to let cool completely.

8. If desired, when the macaroons are cool, place the chocolate in a microwave-safe bowl and microwave on high for 1 minute. Stir thoroughly, then continue to microwave in 20-second increments until all the chocolate is melted and the chocolate feels quite warm (but not hot) when you touch it to your lip. (If you don't have a microwave, melt chocolate in a double boiler.) Drizzle the macaroons with the melted chocolate, and let set on the cooling rack. The macaroons will keep at room temperature for 3 to 5 days, for about 3 weeks in an airtight container in the fridge, and for a few months if stored in an airtight container in the freezer.

stoopid macaroons

rice pudding macaroons

RICE PUDDING *macaroons*

Rice pudding has never been a favorite dessert of mine—it always needs more texture for me. I was never able to get into Jell-O, pudding, flan, custard, or anything else like that. But crème brûlée? Sure thing. Which led me here, to a coconut–rice pudding macaroon that has some texture and crunch to it and won't run through your fingers when you try to pick it up.

Yield: Twenty-four 2-inch macaroons

MACAROONS:

One 14-ounce can sweetened condensed milk
1 cup cooked rice
½ teaspoon vanilla extract
½ teaspoon ground cinnamon, plus extra for garnish
¼ teaspoon ground nutmeg, plus extra for garnish
One 14-ounce bag sweetened shredded coconut
2 large egg whites
¼ teaspoon kosher salt
Unsweetened cocoa powder, for garnish

1. Preheat the oven to 350°F with a rack in the center of the oven. Line a baking sheet with parchment.

2. Add 10½ ounces by weight of the condensed milk to a blender. If you don't have a scale, use approximately 8 ounces (1 cup) by liquid measure. Add the rice, vanilla, cinnamon, and nutmeg and blend until smooth. Transfer to an extra-large bowl, add the coconut, and combine until thoroughly mixed.

3. Add the egg whites and salt to the bowl of a stand mixer (or small bowl if you're using a hand beater) and whip on medium-high until very stiff peaks form, 2½ to 3 minutes.

4. Using a rubber spatula, gently fold the egg whites into the coconut mixture. After it's combined, push the mixture into one big blob to make it easier for you to portion out the macaroons.

5. Dip 2 spoons into a small bowl of water, shake them off, form the mixture into balls approximately 1½ inches in diameter, and place them on the baking sheet about 1 inch apart. (You can also form them by hand, but be sure to wet your fingers frequently.)

6. Place the sheet into the oven and set your timer for 24 minutes. After about 19 minutes, start checking for coloring. Look for an even, light golden color and for the undersides to be nicely tanned. These macaroons will darken a bit more quickly than normal, so keep a close eye on them.

7. Remove from the oven and let the sheet rest on a cooling rack, leaving the macaroons on the sheet until they're cool enough for you to pull off (about 2 minutes depending on how sensitive your fingers are). Transfer the macaroons to the cooling rack to let cool completely.

8. Garnish with a light dusting of cocoa powder, cinnamon, and/or nutmeg before serving. The macaroons will keep at room temperature for 3 to 5 days, for about 3 weeks in an airtight container in the fridge, and for a few months if stored in an airtight container in the freezer.

maple-pecan pie macaroons

MAPLE–PECAN PIE *macaroons*

I love fruit pies. Custard, chocolate, and sugary, buttery pies don't generally appeal to me. Except for pecan pie. I think a good piece of pecan pie is awesome. As they say in France, even a good piece of pecan pie is a great piece of pecan pie. So I figured, why not make a macaroon out of it? And the result is a smooth, nutty morsel of appropriated pecan pie that will make you wonder why you didn't make these first. Unless you did make these first. In which case, you're smarter than you look. I'm kidding. I can't see you. As far as you know.

Yield: Twenty-four 2-inch macaroons

MACAROONS:

One 14-ounce can sweetened condensed milk

2½ ounces (scant 1 cup) pecans, toasted (see Note page 76) and chopped

3 ounces (⅜ cup) dark maple syrup

1 ounce (1 packed tablespoon) dark brown sugar

1 teaspoon unsulfured molasses

½ teaspoon vanilla extract

One 14-ounce bag sweetened shredded coconut

2 large egg whites

¼ teaspoon kosher salt

1. Preheat the oven to 350°F with a rack in the center of the oven. Line a baking sheet with parchment.

2. In an extra-large bowl, measure out 7 ounces by weight of the condensed milk. If you don't have a scale, use approximately 5⅓ ounces (⅔ cup) by liquid measure. Add the pecans, maple syrup, brown sugar, molasses, and vanilla and incorporate with a rubber spatula. Add 12½ ounces of the coconut to the condensed milk mixture and combine until thoroughly mixed.

3. Add the egg whites and salt to the bowl of a stand mixer (or small bowl if you're using a hand beater) and whip on medium-high until very stiff peaks form, 2½ to 3 minutes.

4. Using a rubber spatula, gently fold the whipped egg whites into the coconut mixture. After it's combined, push the mixture into one big blob to make it easier for you to portion out the macaroons.

5. Dip 2 spoons into a small bowl of water, shake them off, form the mixture into balls approximately 1½ inches in diameter, and place them on the baking sheet about 1 inch apart. (You can also form them by hand, but be sure to wet your fingers frequently.)

6. Place the sheet into the oven to bake for 20 to 25 minutes. After about 22 minutes, start checking for coloring. Look for an even, light golden color and for the undersides to be nicely tanned.

7. Remove from the oven and let the sheet rest on a cooling rack, leaving the macaroons on the sheet until they're cool enough for you to pull off (about 2 minutes depending on how sensitive your fingers are). Transfer

the macaroons to the cooling rack to let cool completely. The macaroons will keep at room temperature for 3 to 5 days, for about 3 weeks in an airtight container in the fridge, and for a few months if stored in an airtight container in the freezer.

spiced pumpkin macaroons

SPICED PUMPKIN *macaroons*

You can credit Starbucks for these. I think it's impossible to escape the autumn without passing a sign for a spiced pumpkin latte or some such beverage. But even if you don't know what Starbucks is, what's not to like about creamy pumpkin, cinnamon, cloves, and some crunchy toasted pumpkin seeds? I'll tell you: nothing.

Yield: Twenty-four 2-inch macaroons

MACAROONS:

One 14-ounce can sweetened condensed milk
One 14-ounce can pumpkin puree (if pumpkin isn't available, you can substitute 1 baked sweet potato, skin discarded— about ⅓ cup)
¼ cup raw pepitas (pumpkin seeds)
1 teaspoon vanilla extract
¼ teaspoon ground cinnamon
⅛ teaspoon ground nutmeg (or 15 passes of a whole nutmeg over a grater)
Pinch of ground cloves
One 14-ounce bag sweetened shredded coconut
2 large egg whites
¼ teaspoon kosher salt

1. Preheat the oven to 350°F with a rack in the center of the oven. Line a baking sheet with parchment.

2. In an extra-large bowl, measure out 7 ounces by weight of the condensed milk. If you don't have a scale, use approximately 5⅓ ounces (⅔ cup) by liquid measure. Add 2½ ounces of pumpkin puree by weight, the pepitas (save some for decorating the tops of the macaroons if you'd like), vanilla, cinnamon, nutmeg, and cloves and combine thoroughly with a rubber spatula. Add the coconut to the condensed milk mixture and combine until thoroughly mixed.

3. Add the egg whites and salt to the bowl of a stand mixer (or small bowl if you're using a hand beater) and whip on medium-high until very stiff peaks form, 2½ to 3 minutes.

4. Using a rubber spatula, gently fold the egg whites into the coconut mixture. After it's combined, push the mixture into one big blob to make it easier for you to portion out the macaroons.

5. Dip 2 spoons into a small bowl of water, shake them off, form the mixture into balls approximately 1½ inches in diameter, and place them on the baking sheet about 1 inch apart. (You can also form them by hand, but be sure to wet your fingers frequently.) Top with the reserved pepitas, if you're doing that.

6. Place the sheet into the oven to bake for 20 to 25 minutes. After about 22 minutes, start checking for coloring. Look for nice, even, tanning with little wisps of dark brown coconut.

7. Remove from the oven and let the sheet rest on a cooling rack, leaving the macaroons on the sheet until they're cool enough for you to pull off (about 2 minutes depending on how sensitive your fingers are). Transfer

the macaroons to the cooling rack to let cool completely. The macaroons will keep at room temperature for 3 to 5 days, for about 3 weeks in an airtight container in the fridge, and for a few months if stored in an airtight container in the freezer. These are particularly moist, so if you want to crisp them up again, just pop them into a 350°F oven for 7 to 10 minutes and they'll be like new.

chocolate-banana-nut macaroons

CHOCOLATE-BANANA-NUT
macaroons

Growing up, my favorite desserts were coffee ice cream and chocolate-banana shakes. I had to stop drinking the shakes because I couldn't handle the milk anymore (but surprisingly I could still deal with ice cream*), and that made me sad. I was sad for a long time until I said to myself, "Danny! Stop being sad! Put bananas and chocolate into the macaroons!" It wasn't quite that simple, but these macaroons make me very happy. I think they'll make you happy, too.

Yield: Twenty-four 2-inch macaroons

MACAROONS:

One 14-ounce can sweetened condensed milk

½ ounce (by weight) hazelnut paste (or scant ¼ cup hazelnuts, finely ground)

½ teaspoon vanilla extract

1 ripe (but not black) banana
One 14-ounce bag sweetened shredded coconut

2 large egg whites

¼ teaspoon kosher salt

4 ounces chocolate of your choice, coarsely chopped into pieces the size of a quarter

½ cup walnuts, toasted (see Note page 79) and coarsely chopped

1. Preheat the oven to 350°F with a rack in the center of the oven. Line a baking sheet with parchment.

2. In an extra-large bowl, measure out 10½ ounces by weight of the condensed milk. If you don't have a scale, use approximately 8 ounces (1 cup) by liquid measure. Add the hazelnut paste (or ground hazelnuts) and vanilla and incorporate with a rubber spatula. Add half of the banana, mash with a fork, and stir to combine. Taste the mixture; if the banana flavor isn't strong enough, add more banana in ½-inch slices. When the banana flavor is strong enough for you, add the coconut and combine until thoroughly mixed.

3. Add the egg whites and salt to the bowl of a stand mixer (or small bowl if you're using a hand beater) and whip on medium-high until very stiff peaks form, 2½ to 3 minutes.

4. Using a rubber spatula, gently fold the egg whites into the coconut mixture. After it's combined, push the mixture into one big blob to make it easier for you to portion out the macaroons.

5. Dip 2 spoons into a small bowl of water, shake them off, form the mixture into balls approximately 1½ inches in diameter, and place them on the baking sheet about 1 inch apart. (You can also form them by hand, but be sure to wet your fingers frequently.)

6. Place the sheet into the oven to bake for 20 to 25 minutes. After about 22 minutes, start checking for coloring. Look for an even, light golden color and for the undersides to be nicely tanned.

*And cheese and yogurt, in case you're keeping track.

7. Remove from the oven and let the sheet rest on a cooling rack, leaving the macaroons on the sheet until they're cool enough for you to pull off (about 2 minutes depending on how sensitive your fingers are). Transfer the macaroons to the cooling rack to let cool completely.

8. When the macaroons are cool, place the chocolate in a microwave-safe bowl and microwave on high for 1 minute. Stir thoroughly, then continue to microwave in 20-second increments until all the chocolate is melted and the chocolate feels quite warm (but not hot) when you touch it to your lip. Then spoon or drizzle the chocolate on top of each of the macaroons. Alternatively, you can dip the tops of each macaroon in chocolate. Or the bottoms. Or stick a skewer into each macaroon and completely cloak it. Knock yourself out. Sprinkle with the chopped toasted walnuts.

9. Place back on the cooling rack and wait for the chocolate to set, or place the macaroons in the fridge for 15 to 30 minutes to greatly speed up the process.

10. The macaroons will keep uncovered for 3 to 5 days, for about 3 weeks in an airtight container in the fridge, and for a few months if stored in an airtight container in the freezer.

gingersnap macaroons

GINGERSNAP *macaroons*

Bring these to your next holiday party and be a hero.

Yield: Twenty-four 2-inch macaroons

MACAROONS:

- One 14-ounce can sweetened condensed milk
- 1 tablespoon unsulfured molasses
- 1 ounce (scant ¼ cup) candied ginger
- ¼ teaspoon ground ginger
- ¼ teaspoon vanilla extract
- ¼ teaspoon ground cinnamon
- One 14-ounce bag sweetened shredded coconut
- 2 large egg whites
- ¼ teaspoon kosher salt

1. Preheat the oven to 350°F with a rack in the center of the oven. Line a baking sheet with parchment.

2. Add 10½ ounces by weight of the condensed milk to a blender. If you don't have a scale, use approximately 8 ounces (1 cup) by liquid measure. Add the molasses, candied ginger, ground ginger, vanilla, and cinnamon to the blender and blend until smooth; it may still have some ginger chunks and that's OK. Pour into an extra-large bowl, add the coconut, and combine until thoroughly mixed.

3. Add the egg whites and salt to the bowl of a stand mixer (or small bowl if you're using a hand beater) and whip on medium-high until very stiff peaks form, 2½ to 3 minutes.

4. Using a rubber spatula, gently fold the egg whites into the coconut mixture. After it's combined, push the mixture into one big blob to make it easier for you to portion out the macaroons.

5. Dip 2 spoons into a small bowl of water, shake them off, form the mixture into balls approximately 1½ inches in diameter, and place them on the baking sheet about 1 inch apart. (You can also form them by hand, but be sure to wet your fingers frequently.)

6. Place the sheet into the oven to bake for 20 to 25 minutes. After about 22 minutes, start checking for coloring. Look for an even, light golden color and for the undersides to be nicely tanned.

7. Remove from the oven and let the sheet rest on a cooling rack, leaving the macaroons on the sheet until they're cool enough for you to pull off (about 2 minutes depending on how sensitive your fingers are). Transfer the macaroons to the cooling rack to let cool completely. The macaroons will keep at room temperature for 3 to 5 days, for about 3 weeks in an airtight container in the fridge, and for a few months if stored in an airtight container in the freezer.

COCONUT S'MORES *macaroons*

If we think about coconut macaroons as American macaroons (it's unclear if they should be called that, but let's go with it for this recipe), and if we're making American macaroon sandwiches, why wouldn't we make s'mores? After all, there's no more classically American dessert sandwich than the s'more. These are even better than you think they'll be.

Yield: Twelve 2½-inch maca-roon sandwiches

MACAROONS:

- 1 batch Original Macaroon Sandwich Shells (page 142)
- 6 ounces dark chocolate, chopped
- ½ cup heavy cream
- 4 ounces Marshmallow Fluff or other marshmallow crème (see Note below)
- 1 package graham crackers

1. To make the ganache, place the chocolate into a large bowl. Heat the heavy cream in a large saucepan until very hot but not boiling. Remove from the heat, add the cream to the chocolate, and whisk until fully incorporated and smooth, about 3 minutes. Place in the fridge for 30 minutes or until it firms up (but isn't hardened).

2. While the ganache cools, spread Marshmallow Fluff on half of the shells. If desired, place the marshmallow-topped halves under the broiler for 2 to 3 minutes or until the marshmallow is toasted, or toast with a mini kitchen torch.

3. When the ganache is cool, spread it on the other half of the shells. Place a piece of graham cracker on top of the ganache halves. Close the sandwiches and enjoy.

Variations for the Filling:

Peanut butter and toasted marshmallow

Peanut butter and grape jelly

Raspberry jam

Nutella

Chestnut cream

Key lime curd

note To make your own marshmallow crème, place marshmallows in a microwave-safe bowl and microwave on high in 8-second intervals until the marshmallows can be stirred into a crème.

coconut s'mores macaroons

ginger-coriander macaroons

GINGER-CORIANDER *macaroons*

Please make these if you like ginger. They are so unexpectedly delicious that you just might do a little dance.

Yield: Twenty-four 2-inch macaroons

MACAROONS:

One 14-ounce can
  sweetened condensed milk
2½ ounces (½ cup) candied ginger
½ teaspoon ground coriander
¼ teaspoon vanilla extract
One 14-ounce bag
  sweetened shredded
  coconut
2 large egg whites
¼ teaspoon kosher salt

1. Preheat the oven to 350°F with a rack in the center of the oven. Line a baking sheet with parchment.

2. Add 10½ ounces by weight of the condensed milk to a blender. If you don't have a scale, use approximately 8 ounces (1 cup) by liquid measure. Add the ginger, coriander, and vanilla to the blender and blend until smooth; it may still have some ginger chunks and that's OK. Pour into an extra-large bowl, add the coconut, and combine until thoroughly mixed.

3. Add the egg whites and salt to the bowl of a stand mixer (or small bowl if you're using a hand beater) and whip on medium-high until very stiff peaks form, 2½ to 3 minutes.

4. Using a rubber spatula, gently fold the egg whites into the coconut mixture. After it's combined, push the mixture into one big blob to make it easier for you to portion out the macaroons.

5. Dip 2 spoons into a small bowl of water, shake them off, form the mixture into balls approximately 1½ inches in diameter, and place them on the baking sheet about 1 inch apart. (You can also form them by hand, but be sure to wet your fingers frequently.)

6. Place the sheet into the oven to bake for 20 to 25 minutes. After about 22 minutes, start checking for coloring. Look for an even, light golden color and for the undersides to be nicely tanned.

7. Remove from the oven and let the sheet rest on a cooling rack, leaving the macaroons on the sheet until they're cool enough for you to pull off (about 2 minutes depending on how sensitive your fingers are). Transfer the macaroons to the cooling rack to let cool completely. The macaroons will keep at room temperature for 3 to 5 days, for about 3 weeks in an airtight container in the fridge, and for a few months if stored in an airtight container in the freezer.

CHOCOLATE-CHERRY *macaroons*

If you're one of those people with a liquor cabinet full of strange things—or, if your grandparents have weird stuff lying around that you can't imagine ever drinking—it's entirely possible that you've got some cherry liqueur on hand. One fantastic way to use some of it is in these macaroons. You'll be amazed at what happens when these flavors come together: Bright, tart cherry contrasted with toasted coconut and rounded out by deep, dark chocolate all work to create something very, very special.

Yield: Twenty-four 2-inch macaroons

MACAROONS:

One 14-ounce can
   sweetened condensed milk
2 ounces (½ cup) dried
   cherries, plus 24 for topping
   (optional)
1 tablespoon cherry liqueur
2 teaspoons unsweetened
   cocoa powder
½ teaspoon vanilla extract
One 14-ounce bag
   sweetened shredded
   coconut
2 large egg whites
¼ teaspoon kosher salt
   Optional:
   4 ounces chocolate of your
   choice, coarsely chopped
   into pieces the size of a
   quarter

1. Preheat the oven to 350°F with a rack in the center of the oven. Line a baking sheet with parchment.

2. Add 10½ ounces by weight of the condensed milk to a blender. If you don't have a scale, use approximately 8 ounces (1 cup) by liquid measure. Add the cherries, cherry liqueur, cocoa powder, and vanilla to the blender and blend until fully combined. Pour into an extra-large bowl. Add the coconut and combine until thoroughly mixed.

3. Add the egg whites and salt to the bowl of a stand mixer (or small bowl if you're using a hand beater) and whip on medium-high until very stiff peaks form, 2½ to 3 minutes.

4. Using a rubber spatula, gently fold the whipped egg whites into the coconut mixture. After it's combined, push the mixture into one big blob to make it easier for you to portion out the macaroons.

5. Dip 2 spoons into a small bowl of water, shake them off, form the mixture into balls approximately 1½ inches in diameter, and place them on the baking sheet about 1 inch apart. (You can also form them by hand, but be sure to wet your fingers frequently.)

6. Place the sheet into the oven to bake for 20 to 25 minutes. After about 22 minutes, start checking for coloring. Look for an even, light golden color and for the undersides to be nicely tanned.

7. Remove from the oven and let the sheet rest on a cooling rack, leaving the macaroons on the sheet until they're cool enough for you to pull off (about 2 minutes depending on how sensitive your fingers are). Transfer the macaroons to the cooling rack to let cool completely.

chocolate-cherry macaroons

8. If desired, when the macaroons are cool, place the chocolate in a microwave-safe bowl and microwave on high for 1 minute. Stir thoroughly, then continue to microwave in 20-second increments until all the chocolate is melted and the chocolate feels quite warm (but not hot) when you touch it to your lip. Then spoon or drizzle the chocolate on top of each of the macaroons. Alternatively, you can dip the tops of each macaroon in chocolate. Or the bottoms. Or stick a skewer into each macaroon and completely cloak it. Knock yourself out. Top each with a single dried cherry, if desired. Place back on the cooling rack and wait for the chocolate to set, or place the macaroons in the fridge for 15 to 30 minutes to greatly speed up the process.

9. The macaroons will keep at room temperature for 3 to 5 days, for about 3 weeks in an airtight container in the fridge, and for a few months if stored in an airtight container in the freezer.

"BRIGHT, TART CHERRY
contrasted with

Toasted Coconut
AND
rounded out by deep,
DARK CHOCOLATE
ALL WORK TO CREATE SOMETHING
very, very special."

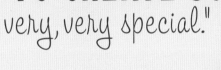

APRICOT *macaroons*

This recipe was inspired by a conversation I had one afternoon while selling macaroons at Smorgasburg, one of the best-known artisanal product markets in the country, which is held in Brooklyn. A customer came up and told me that she, too, made delicious macaroons but that she put chunks of dried apricots in hers and that everyone loved them. I prefer a smoother base to the macaroon than that, so I've recommended blending the apricots in with the condensed milk, but do what suits you. And always remember that you never do know where inspiration will come from.

Yield: Twenty-four 2-inch macaroons

MACAROONS:

One 14-ounce can sweetened condensed milk
2½ ounces (¼ cup) dried apricots
½ teaspoon vanilla extract
One 14-ounce bag sweetened shredded coconut
2 large egg whites
¼ teaspoon kosher salt
Optional:
¼ cup walnuts, toasted (see Note page 79) and chopped

1. Preheat the oven to 350°F with a rack in the center of the oven. Line a baking sheet with parchment.

2. Add 8 ounces of the condensed milk by weight to a blender. If you don't have a scale, use approximately 6 ounces (¾ cup) by liquid measure. Add the apricots and vanilla and blend on high until the apricots are fully incorporated (or substantially incorporated if you'd like some chunks). Pour the condensed milk mixture into an extra-large bowl, add the coconut, and combine until thoroughly mixed.

3. Add the egg whites and salt to the bowl of a stand mixer (or small bowl if you're using a hand beater) and whip on medium-high until very stiff peaks form, 2½ to 3 minutes.

4. Using a rubber spatula, gently fold the egg whites into the coconut mixture. After it's combined, push the mixture into one big blob to make it easier for you to portion out the macaroons.

5. Dip 2 spoons into a small bowl of water, shake them off, form the mixture into balls approximately 1½ inches in diameter, and place them on the baking sheet about 1 inch apart. (You can also form them by hand, but be sure to wet your fingers frequently.) If desired, sprinkle the chopped walnuts onto each macaroon.

6. Place the sheet into the oven to bake for 20 to 25 minutes. After about 22 minutes, start checking for coloring. Look for an even, light golden color and for the undersides to be nicely tanned.

7. Remove from the oven and let the sheet rest on a cooling rack, leaving the macaroons on the sheet until they're cool enough for you to pull off

apricot macaroons

(about 2 minutes depending on how sensitive your fingers are). Transfer the macaroons to the cooling rack to let cool completely. The macaroons will keep at room temperature for 3 to 5 days, for about 3 weeks in an airtight container in the fridge, and for a few months if stored in an airtight container in the freezer.

HIBISCUS *macaroons*

Hibiscus flowers produce a tea that's tart and refreshing. They're a common ingredient in Latin summertime beverages, and the flowers can often be found at Mexican or Latin-American markets as well as specialty retailers. You can drink the tea hot or make it iced, or, as in this recipe, reduce it down, add some confectioners' sugar, and make one of the most beautiful glazes you'll ever see. Thank you, Fany Gerson (La Newyorkina)!

Yield: Twenty-four 2-inch macaroons

MACAROONS:

- 2 tablespoons dried hibiscus flowers
- One 14-ounce can sweetened condensed milk
- One 14-ounce bag sweetened shredded coconut
- 2 large egg whites
- ¼ teaspoon kosher salt
- 1 to 2 cups confectioners' sugar

1. In a medium pot, bring 2 cups of water to a boil. Add the hibiscus flowers to the boiling water to steep for 10 minutes, then remove from the heat and let steep for 10 more minutes. Pour the tea through a strainer. Set aside ½ cup of the tea, add the rest back to the pot, and return the pot to the heat. Simmer until the tea has reduced to about ¼ cup. Set the reduction aside.

2. Preheat the oven to 350°F with a rack in the center of the oven. Line a baking sheet with parchment.

3. In an extra-large bowl, measure 10½ ounces by weight of the condensed milk. If you don't have a scale, use approximately 8 ounces (1 cup) by liquid measure. Add the hibiscus reduction and stir to combine. Add the coconut and combine until thoroughly mixed.

4. Add the egg whites and salt to the bowl of a stand mixer (or small bowl if you're using a hand beater) and whip on medium-high until very stiff peaks form, 2½ to 3 minutes.

5. Using a rubber spatula, gently fold the egg whites into the coconut mixture. After it's combined, push the mixture into one big blob to make it easier for you to portion out the macaroons.

6. Dip 2 spoons into a small bowl of water, shake them off, form the mixture into balls approximately 1½ inches in diameter, and place them on the baking sheet about 1 inch apart. (You can also form them by hand, but be sure to wet your fingers frequently.)

7. Place the sheet into the oven to bake for 20 to 25 minutes. After about 22 minutes, start checking for coloring. Look for an even, light golden

hibiscus macaroons

color and for the undersides to be nicely tanned.

8. Remove from the oven and let the sheet rest on a cooling rack, leaving the macaroons on the sheet until they're cool enough for you to pull off (about 2 minutes depending on how sensitive your fingers are). Transfer the macaroons to the cooling rack to let cool completely.

9. Place the reserved ½ cup hibiscus tea in a small bowl and, while continuously stirring, slowly add the confectioners' sugar until the glaze thickens. Since you'll be drizzling the glaze onto the macaroons, it's up to you to decide how thick you'd like your glaze. Use less sugar if you'd like a translucent glaze and more sugar if you'd like it to be more opaque. When it's to your liking, drizzle away.

10. The macaroons will keep at room temperature for 3 to 5 days, for about 3 weeks in an airtight container in the fridge, and for a few months if stored in an airtight container in the freezer. If you're going to freeze them, it's better to store them unglazed and then glaze before serving.

CHOCOLATE-RASPBERRY
macaroons

These are sinfully delicious and quite beautiful. If you want to be the star of wherever you bring these, hide a raspberry in the center of each one. I promise you that at least one person will say, "Oh, how nice." You can use frozen raspberries for the 4 ounces, but fresh ones are much better for the raspberries to be inserted into the macaroons, if you're doing so.

Yield: Twenty-four 2-inch macaroons

MACAROONS:

    One 14-ounce can sweetened condensed milk

4 ounces (1 cup) fresh raspberries, plus 24 fresh raspberries (optional)

½ teaspoon vanilla extract

    One 14-ounce bag sweetened shredded coconut

2 large egg whites

¼ teaspoon kosher salt

4 ounces chocolate of your choice, coarsely chopped into pieces the size of a quarter

1. Preheat the oven to 350°F with a rack in the center of the oven. Line a baking sheet with parchment.

2. In an extra-large bowl, measure out 10½ ounces by weight of the condensed milk. If you don't have a scale, use approximately 8 ounces (1 cup) by liquid measure. Add the 4 ounces raspberries and the vanilla. Incorporate with a rubber spatula, taking care to keep the raspberries as intact as possible. Add the coconut to the condensed milk mixture and combine until thoroughly mixed. You're going to continue to break apart the raspberries, but just try to be as gentle as possible.

3. Add the egg whites and salt to the bowl of a stand mixer (or small bowl if you're using a hand beater) and whip on medium-high until very stiff peaks form, 2½ to 3 minutes.

4. Using a rubber spatula, gently fold the whipped egg whites into the coconut mixture. After it's combined, push the mixture into one big blob to make it easier for you to portion out the macaroons.

5. Dip 2 spoons into a small bowl of water, shake them off, form the mixture into balls approximately 1½ inches in diameter, and place them on the baking sheet about 1 inch apart. (You can also form them by hand, but be sure to wet your fingers frequently.) Make a small well in each macaroon and place a single raspberry in each well, if desired. Fold the sides of each macaroon up to fully enclose the raspberry.

6. Place the sheet into the oven to bake for 20 to 25 minutes. After about 22 minutes, start checking for coloring. Look for an even, light golden color and for the undersides to be nicely tanned.

7. Remove from the oven and let the sheet rest on a cooling rack, leaving the macaroons on the sheet until they're cool enough for you to pull off (about 2 minutes depending on how sensitive your fingers are). Transfer the macaroons to the cooling rack to let cool completely.

8. When the macaroons are cool, place the chocolate in a microwave-safe bowl and microwave on high for 1 minute. Stir thoroughly, then continue to microwave in 20-second increments until all the chocolate is melted and the chocolate feels quite warm (but not hot) when you touch it to your lip. Then spoon or drizzle the chocolate on top of each of the macaroons. Alternatively, you can dip the tops of each macaroon in chocolate. Or the bottoms. Or stick a skewer into each macaroon and completely cloak it. Knock yourself out.

9. Place back on the cooling rack and wait for the chocolate to set, or place the macaroons in the fridge for 15 to 30 minutes to greatly speed up the process. The macaroons will keep at room temperature for 3 to 5 days, for about 3 weeks in an airtight container in the fridge, and for a few months if stored in an airtight container in the freezer.

SUNSHINE *macaroons*

This is one of those things that people generally refer to as a happy accident. I was trying to make a macaroon using a wheat beer but in the process wound up with a delicate, citrusy, and wonderfully pleasant macaroon. They are bright, summery treats that work well in the mornings.

Yield: Twenty-four 2-inch macaroons

MACAROONS:

- One 14-ounce can sweetened condensed milk
- ½ teaspoon vanilla extract
- Grated zest of 1 lemon
- Grated zest of ½ orange
- One 14-ounce bag sweetened shredded coconut
- 2 large egg whites
- ¼ teaspoon kosher salt

1. Preheat the oven to 350°F with a rack in the center of the oven. Line a baking sheet with parchment.

2. In an extra-large bowl, measure out 10½ ounces by weight of the condensed milk. If you don't have a scale, use approximately 8 ounces (1 cup) by liquid measure. Add the vanilla and both zests. Incorporate with a rubber spatula. Add the coconut to the condensed milk mixture and combine until thoroughly mixed.

3. Add the egg whites and salt to the bowl of a stand mixer (or small bowl if you're using a hand beater) and whip on medium-high until very stiff peaks form, 2½ to 3 minutes.

4. Using a rubber spatula, gently fold the egg whites into the coconut mixture. After it's combined, push the mixture into one big blob to make it easier for you to portion out the macaroons.

5. Dip 2 spoons into a small bowl of water, shake them off, form the mixture into balls approximately 1½ inches in diameter, and place them on the baking sheet about 1 inch apart. (You can also form them by hand, but be sure to wet your fingers frequently.)

6. Place the sheet into the oven to bake for 20 to 25 minutes. After about 22 minutes, start checking for coloring. Look for an even, light golden color and for the undersides to be nicely tanned.

7. Remove from the oven and let the sheet rest on a cooling rack, leaving the macaroons on the sheet until they're cool enough for you to pull off (about 2 minutes depending on how sensitive your fingers are). Transfer the macaroons to the cooling rack to let cool completely. The macaroons will keep at room temperature for 3 to 5 days, for about 3 weeks in an airtight container in the fridge, and for a few months if stored in an airtight container in the freezer.

sunshine macaroons

domino macaroons

DOMINO macaroons

These are named for the group of Dominican men and women in my neighborhood who play dominoes outside day-in and day-out and who particularly enjoy this flavor.

Yield: Twenty-four 2-inch macaroons

MACAROONS:

  One 14-ounce can sweetened condensed milk
1 teaspoon grated fresh ginger
½ teaspoon ground cinnamon
½ teaspoon vanilla extract
  One 14-ounce bag sweetened shredded coconut
2 large egg whites
¼ teaspoon kosher salt

1. Preheat the oven to 350°F with a rack in the center of the oven. Line a baking sheet with parchment.

2. In an extra-large bowl, measure out 10½ ounces by weight of the condensed milk. If you don't have a scale, use approximately 8 ounces (1 cup) by liquid measure. Add the ginger, cinnamon, and vanilla. Incorporate with a rubber spatula. Add the coconut to the condensed milk mixture and combine until thoroughly mixed.

3. Add the egg whites and salt to the bowl of a stand mixer (or small bowl if you're using a hand beater) and whip on medium-high until very stiff peaks form, 2½ to 3 minutes.

4. Using a rubber spatula, gently fold the egg whites into the coconut mixture. After it's combined, push the mixture into one big blob to make it easier for you to portion out the macaroons.

5. Dip 2 spoons into a small bowl of water, shake them off, form the mixture into balls approximately 1½ inches in diameter, and place them on the baking sheet about 1 inch apart. (You can also form them by hand, but be sure to wet your fingers frequently.)

6. Place the sheet into the oven to bake for 20 to 25 minutes. After about 22 minutes, start checking for coloring. Look for an even, light golden color and for the undersides to be nicely tanned.

7. Remove from the oven and let the sheet rest on a cooling rack, leaving the macaroons on the sheet until they're cool enough for you to pull off (about 2 minutes depending on how sensitive your fingers are). Transfer the macaroons to the cooling rack to let cool completely. The macaroons will keep at room temperature for 3 to 5 days, for about 3 weeks in an airtight container in the fridge, and for a few months if stored in an airtight container in the freezer.

ESPRESSO *macaroons*

Macaroons pair so well with coffee; that's why they're sold in wonderful coffee shops all over New York. This recipe brings coffee and macaroons together in a most harmonious fashion.

Yield: Twenty-four 2-inch macaroons

MACAROONS:

- One 14-ounce can sweetened condensed milk
- 1¼ teaspoons instant espresso powder
- ¼ teaspoon vanilla extract
- One 14-ounce bag sweetened shredded coconut
- 2 large egg whites
- ¼ teaspoon kosher salt
- Unsweetened cocoa powder, for dusting

1. Preheat the oven to 350°F with a rack in the center of the oven. Line a baking sheet with parchment.

2. In an extra-large bowl, measure out 10½ ounces by weight of the condensed milk. If you don't have a scale, use approximately 8 ounces (1 cup) by liquid measure. Add the instant espresso powder and vanilla and incorporate with a rubber spatula. Add the coconut to the condensed milk mixture and combine until thoroughly mixed.

3. Add the egg whites and salt to the bowl of a stand mixer (or small bowl if you're using a hand beater) and whip on medium-high until very stiff peaks form, 2½ to 3 minutes.

4. Using a rubber spatula, gently fold the egg whites into the coconut mixture. After it's combined, push the mixture into one big blob to make it easier for you to portion out the macaroons.

5. Dip 2 spoons into a small bowl of water, shake them off, form the mixture into balls approximately 1½ inches in diameter, and place them on the baking sheet about 1 inch apart. (You can also form them by hand, but be sure to wet your fingers frequently.)

6. Place the sheet into the oven to bake for 20 to 25 minutes. After about 22 minutes, start checking for coloring. Look for an even darkening of the macaroons.

7. Remove from the oven and let the sheet rest on a cooling rack, leaving the macaroons on the sheet until they're cool enough for you to pull off (about 2 minutes depending on how sensitive your fingers are). Transfer the macaroons to the cooling rack to let cool completely. The macaroons will keep at room temperature for 3 to 5 days, for about 3 weeks in an airtight container in the fridge, and for a few months if stored in an airtight container in the freezer.

8. Before serving, lightly dust with cocoa powder.

espresso macaroons

cappuccino macaroons

CAPPUCCINO *macaroons*

I used to love cappuccinos. LOVE them. Then drinking milk became problematic, but the combination of coffee, milk, and cinnamon is still delicious. Feel free to serve these with a whipped cream chaser if you so desire.

Yield: Twenty-four 2-inch macaroons

MACAROONS:

One 14-ounce can sweetened condensed milk

1¼ teaspoons instant espresso powder

¼ teaspoon ground cinnamon

¼ teaspoon vanilla extract

One 14-ounce bag sweetened shredded coconut

2 large egg whites

¼ teaspoon kosher salt

Optional:

Extra ground cinnamon and/or unsweetened cocoa powder, for dusting

1. Preheat the oven to 350°F with a rack in the center of the oven. Line a baking sheet with parchment.

2. In an extra-large bowl, measure out 10½ ounces by weight of the condensed milk. If you don't have a scale, use approximately 8 ounces (1 cup) by liquid measure. Add the instant espresso powder, cinnamon, and vanilla and incorporate with a rubber spatula. Add the coconut to the condensed milk mixture and combine until thoroughly mixed.

3. Add the egg whites and salt to the bowl of a stand mixer (or small bowl if you're using a hand beater) and whip on medium-high until very stiff peaks form, 2½ to 3 minutes.

4. Using a rubber spatula, gently fold the egg whites into the coconut mixture. After it's combined, push the mixture into one big blob to make it easier for you to portion out the macaroons.

5. Dip 2 spoons into a small bowl of water, shake them off, form the mixture into balls approximately 1½ inches in diameter, and place them on the baking sheet about 1 inch apart. (You can also form them by hand, but be sure to wet your fingers frequently.)

6. Place the sheet into the oven to bake for 20 to 25 minutes. After about 22 minutes, start checking for coloring. Look for an even darkening of the macaroons.

7. Remove from the oven and transfer the macaroons to a cooling rack to let cool completely. The macaroons will keep at room temperature for 3 to 5 days, for about 3 weeks in an airtight container in the fridge, and for a few months if stored in an airtight container in the freezer.

8. If desired, before serving, dust with cinnamon and/or cocoa powder.

MOCHA *macaroons*

If we're going to have an espresso macaroon, we may as well have all of its friends from the coffee shop menu.

Yield: Twenty-four 2-inch macaroons

MACAROONS:

One 14-ounce can sweetened condensed milk
1 tablespoon unsweetened cocoa powder, plus extra for dusting
1¼ teaspoons instant espresso powder
One 14-ounce bag sweetened shredded coconut
2 large egg whites
¼ teaspoon kosher salt

1. Preheat the oven to 350°F with a rack in the center of the oven. Line a baking sheet with parchment.

2. In an extra-large bowl, measure out 10½ ounces by weight of the condensed milk. If you don't have a scale, use approximately 8 ounces (1 cup) by liquid measure. Add the cocoa powder and instant espresso powder and incorporate with a rubber spatula. Add the coconut to the condensed milk mixture and combine until thoroughly mixed.

3. Add the egg whites and salt to the bowl of a stand mixer (or small bowl if you're using a hand beater) and whip on medium-high until very stiff peaks form, 2½ to 3 minutes.

4. Using a rubber spatula, gently fold the egg whites into the coconut mixture. After it's combined, push the mixture into one big blob to make it easier for you to portion out the macaroons.

5. Dip 2 spoons into a small bowl of water, shake them off, form the mixture into balls approximately 1½ inches in diameter, and place them on the baking sheet about 1 inch apart. (You can also form them by hand, but be sure to wet your fingers frequently.)

6. Place the sheet into the oven to bake for 20 to 25 minutes. After about 22 minutes, start checking for coloring. Look for an even darkening of the macaroons.

7. Remove from the oven and let the sheet rest on a cooling rack, leaving the macaroons on the sheet until they're cool enough for you to pull off (about 2 minutes depending on how sensitive your fingers are). Transfer the macaroons to the cooling rack to let cool completely. The macaroons will keep at room temperature for 3 to 5 days, for about 3 weeks in an airtight container in the fridge, and for a few months if stored in an airtight container in the freezer.

8. Before serving, lightly dust with cocoa powder.

mocha macaroons

pistachio macaroons

PISTACHIO *macaroons*

Pistachios are delicious, macaroons are delicious, and pistachio macarons are delicious. So why shouldn't pistachio macaroons be delicious, too? Turns out, they are! I like to amp up the pistachio taste because pistachios are generally a treat, and when I'm having treats, I like to HAVE TREATS, if you know what I mean.

Yield: Twenty-four 2-inch macaroons

MACAROONS:

One 14-ounce can sweetened condensed milk
1 ounce pistachio paste (if you can't find pistachio paste, grind 1 cup unsalted roasted pistachios until paste-like)
½ teaspoon vanilla extract
One 14-ounce bag sweetened shredded coconut
2 large egg whites
¼ teaspoon kosher salt
¼ cup pistachios, toasted (see Note below) and chopped

1. Preheat the oven to 350°F with a rack in the center of the oven. Line a baking sheet with parchment.

2. In an extra-large bowl, measure out 10½ ounces by weight of the condensed milk. If you don't have a scale, use approximately 8 ounces (1 cup) by liquid measure. Add the pistachio paste and vanilla. Incorporate with a rubber spatula. Add the coconut to the condensed milk mixture and combine until thoroughly mixed.

3. Add the egg whites and salt to the bowl of a stand mixer (or small bowl if you're using a hand beater) and whip on medium-high until very stiff peaks form, 2½ to 3 minutes.

4. Using a rubber spatula, gently fold the egg whites into the coconut mixture. After it's combined, push the mixture into one big blob to make it easier for you to portion out the macaroons.

5. Dip 2 spoons into a small bowl of water, shake them off, form the mixture into balls approximately 1½ inches in diameter, and place them on the baking sheet about 1 inch apart. (You can also form them by hand, but be sure to wet your fingers frequently.) Sprinkle the chopped pistachios onto each macaroon.

6. Place the sheet into the oven to bake for 20 to 25 minutes. After about 22 minutes, start checking for coloring. Look for an even, light golden color and for the undersides to be nicely tanned.

7. Remove from the oven and let the sheet rest on a cooling rack, leaving the macaroons on the sheet until they're cool enough for you to pull off (about 2 minutes depending on how sensitive your fingers are). Transfer the macaroons to the cooling rack to let cool completely. The macaroons will keep at room temperature for 3 to 5 days, for about 3 weeks in an

airtight container in the fridge, and for a few months if stored in an airtight container in the freezer.

note To toast the pistachios, place the pistachios in a single layer on a baking sheet and place into a preheated 350°F oven for 10 to 15 minutes or until fragrant, giving them a shake and a stir halfway through. Remove from the oven and set aside to cool.

"When I'm having treats, I like to

HAVE TREATS,

if you know what I mean."

chestnut-rum macaroons

CHESTNUT-RUM *macaroons*

I don't know anyone who likes chestnuts. Not a single person. I don't even know what you're supposed to do with them besides toasting them over an open flame, and that doesn't even sound that interesting to me. But here's the magic of the macaroon and doing crazy things with macaroons: Just try it. So I tried out some chestnut puree, because, I mean, if it's in a store then that must mean that someone somewhere likes it, right? And you know what? It makes a pretty damn tasty macaroon! These remind me of what Christmas in Minnesota must taste like for Jews.

Yield: Twenty-four 2-inch macaroons

MACAROONS:

- One 14-ounce can sweetened condensed milk
- 3 ounces chestnut puree
- 2 teaspoons dark spiced rum
- ½ teaspoon vanilla extract
- ½ teaspoon unsweetened cocoa powder
- One 14-ounce bag sweetened shredded coconut
- 2 large egg whites
- ¼ teaspoon kosher salt

1. Preheat the oven to 350°F with a rack in the center of the oven. Line a baking sheet with parchment.

2. In an extra-large bowl, measure out 6 ounces by weight of the condensed milk. If you don't have a scale, use approximately 5 ounces (½ cup plus 2 tablespoons) by liquid measure. Add the chestnut puree, rum, vanilla, and cocoa powder and incorporate with a rubber spatula. Add the coconut to the condensed milk mixture and combine until thoroughly mixed.

3. Add the egg whites and salt to the bowl of a stand mixer (or small bowl if you're using a hand beater) and whip on medium-high until very stiff peaks form, 2½ to 3 minutes.

4. Using a rubber spatula, gently fold the egg whites into the coconut mixture. After it's combined, push the mixture into one big blob to make it easier for you to portion out the macaroons.

5. Dip 2 spoons into a small bowl of water, shake them off, form the mixture into balls approximately 1½ inches in diameter, and place them on the baking sheet about 1 inch apart. (You can also form them by hand, but be sure to wet your fingers frequently.)

6. Place the sheet into the oven to bake for 20 to 25 minutes. After about 22 minutes, start checking for coloring. Look for an even, light golden color and for the undersides to be nicely tanned.

7. Remove from the oven and let the sheet rest on a cooling rack, leaving the macaroons on the sheet until they're cool enough for you to pull off

(about 2 minutes depending on how sensitive your fingers are). Transfer the macaroons to the cooling rack to let cool completely. The macaroons will keep at room temperature for 3 to 5 days, for about 3 weeks in an airtight container in the fridge, and for a few months if stored in an airtight container in the freezer.

note Chestnut paste (not the puree used here) makes a GREAT filling for macaroon sandwiches. Make chocolate shells (see page 147) with some chestnut paste and maybe just a dab of a cherry jam. It's a killer in the sweetest of ways.

PEANUT BUTTER & JELLY
macaroons

I made these on a whim one day and was blown away. I generally think that macaroons are best the day after they've been baked, but these macaroons are killer when warm out of the oven. Just delicious little bites of America.

Yield: Twenty-four 2-inch macaroons

MACAROONS:

- One 14-ounce can sweetened condensed milk
- 2½ ounces (¼ cup) smooth peanut butter (or chunky, as you like)
- ⅛ teaspoon vanilla extract
- One 14-ounce bag sweetened shredded coconut
- 2 large egg whites
- ¼ teaspoon kosher salt
- Grape jam, for filling (thicker jam is better than thinner)

1. Preheat the oven to 350°F with a rack in the center of the oven. Line a baking sheet with parchment.

2. In an extra-large bowl, measure out 7 ounces by weight of the condensed milk. If you don't have a scale, use approximately 5⅓ ounces (⅔ cup) by liquid measure. Add the peanut butter and vanilla and incorporate with a rubber spatula. Add the coconut to the condensed milk mixture and combine until thoroughly mixed.

3. Add the egg whites and salt to the bowl of a stand mixer (or small bowl if you're using a hand beater) and whip on medium-high until very stiff peaks form, 2½ to 3 minutes.

4. Using a rubber spatula, gently fold the whipped egg whites into the coconut mixture. After it's combined, push the mixture into one big blob to make it easier for you to portion out the macaroons.

5. Dip 2 spoons into a small bowl of water, shake them off, form the mixture into balls approximately 1½ inches in diameter, and place them on the baking sheet about 1 inch apart. (You can also form them by hand, but be sure to wet your fingers frequently.)

6. Make a well in the center of each macaroon and fill with the grape jam. Fold the sides of each macaroon up and over the jam to hide it in the center. Place the sheet into the oven to bake for 19 to 23 minutes. After about 20 minutes, start checking for coloring. Look for an even, light golden color and for the undersides to be nicely tanned.

7. Remove from the oven and let the sheet rest on a cooling rack, leaving the macaroons on the sheet until they're cool enough for you to pull off (about 2 minutes depending on how sensitive your fingers are). Transfer

peanut butter & jelly macaroons

the macaroons to the cooling rack to let cool completely. The macaroons will keep at room temperature for 3 to 5 days, for about 3 weeks in an airtight container in the fridge, and for a few months if stored in an airtight container in the freezer.

chocolate bombs

CHOCOLATE BOMBS

When I was in seventh or eighth grade, there was a kid named Fritz. Fritz had a brother named Franz. Every Monday, Franz would ask me for $20 and promise to pay me back $40 the following Friday. Sure enough, every Friday Franz would give me $40. I never asked any questions—this went on for months until Franz left school. I still don't know what Franz did with my money or why he doubled it for letting him use it for four days, but I can tell you this: The chocolate ganache inside these macaroons is very much like getting an extra $20 every Friday.

Yield: Twenty-four 2-inch macaroons

MACAROONS:

One 14-ounce can sweetened condensed milk
1 teaspoon vanilla extract
One 14-ounce bag sweetened shredded coconut
2 large egg whites
¼ teaspoon kosher salt
4 ounces chocolate ganache (see Note below)

1. Preheat the oven to 350°F with a rack in the center of the oven. Line a baking sheet with parchment.

2. In an extra-large bowl, measure out 10½ ounces by weight of the condensed milk. If you don't have a scale, use approximately 8 ounces (1 cup) by liquid measure. Add the vanilla and incorporate with a rubber spatula. Add the coconut to the condensed milk mixture and combine until thoroughly mixed.

3. Add the egg whites and salt to the bowl of a stand mixer (or small bowl if you're using a hand beater) and whip on medium-high until very stiff peaks form, 2½ to 3 minutes.

4. Using a rubber spatula, gently fold the whipped egg whites into the coconut mixture. After it's combined, push the mixture into one big blob to make it easier for you to portion out the macaroons.

5. Dip 2 spoons into a small bowl of water, shake them off, form the mixture into balls approximately 1½ inches in diameter, and place them on the baking sheet about 1 inch apart. (You can also form them by hand, but be sure to wet your fingers frequently.)

6. Make a well in the center of each macaroon and fill with the ganache. Fold the sides of each macaroon up and over the ganache to hide it in the center. Place the sheet into the oven to bake for 19 to 23 minutes. After about 20 minutes, start checking for coloring. Look for an even, light golden color and for the undersides to be nicely tanned.

7. Remove from the oven and let the sheet rest on a cooling rack, leaving the macaroons on the sheet until they're cool enough for you to pull off

(about 2 minutes depending on how sensitive your fingers are). Transfer the macaroons to the cooling rack to let cool completely. The macaroons will keep at room temperature for 3 to 5 days, for about 3 weeks in an airtight container in the fridge, and for a few months if stored in an airtight container in the freezer.

note To make the chocolate ganache, add 4 ounces dark chocolate to a large bowl. Heat 3 ounces (6 tablespoons) heavy cream in a saucepan until hot but not boiling. Remove from the heat and pour over the chocolate, whisking constantly until the chocolate is completely melted. Let cool before using. This makes about 7 ounces.

GUAVA *macaroons*

Guava might not be familiar to you. If this is your first time working with it, do yourself a favor and buy two packages of guava paste. Once you taste it, you're likely to eat an entire package before even making the macaroons, like I did. Or maybe you have self-control. What am I, your psychologist?

Yield: Twenty-four 2-inch macaroons

MACAROONS:

One 14-ounce can sweetened condensed milk
One 14-ounce can guava puree
One 14-ounce bag sweetened shredded coconut
2 large egg whites
¼ teaspoon kosher salt
One 14-ounce package guava paste

1. Preheat the oven to 350°F with a rack in the center of the oven. Line a baking sheet with parchment.

2. In an extra-large bowl, measure out 8 ounces of the condensed milk by weight. If you don't have a scale, use approximately half of the can. Add 2 ounces of the guava puree and incorporate with a rubber spatula. Add the coconut and combine until thoroughly mixed.

3. Add the egg whites and salt to the bowl of a stand mixer (or small bowl if you're using a hand beater) and whip on medium-high until very stiff peaks form, 2½ to 3 minutes.

4. Using a rubber spatula, gently fold the egg whites into the coconut mixture. After it's combined, push the mixture into one big blob to make it easier for you to portion out the macaroons.

5. Dip 2 spoons into a small bowl of water, shake them off, form the mixture into balls approximately 1½ inches in diameter, and place them on the baking sheet about 1 inch apart. (You can also form them by hand, but be sure to wet your fingers frequently.)

6. Tear off approximately ½-inch cubes of guava paste and push 1 cube into the center of each macaroon. You can either leave them as "thumbprint" cookies or fold up the surrounding macaroon batter to fully enclose the guava paste. Place the sheet into the oven to bake for 22 minutes. After about 19 minutes, start checking for coloring. Look for an even, light golden color and for the undersides to be nicely tanned.

7. Remove from the oven and let the sheet rest on a cooling rack, leaving the macaroons on the sheet until they're cool enough for you to pull off (about 2 minutes depending on how sensitive your fingers are). Transfer the macaroons to the cooling rack to let cool completely. The macaroons will keep at room temperature for 3 to 5 days, for about 3 weeks in an

guava macaroons

airtight container in the fridge, and for a few months if stored in an airtight container in the freezer.

raspberry macaroons

RASPBERRY *macaroons*

Find your favorite raspberry jam and have yourself a raspberry party.

Yield: Twenty-four 2-inch macaroons

MACAROONS:

- One 14-ounce can sweetened condensed milk
- 2 ounces (½ cup) fresh raspberries
- ½ teaspoon vanilla extract
- Grated zest of ½ lemon
- One 14-ounce bag sweetened shredded coconut
- 2 large egg whites
- ¼ teaspoon kosher salt
- Raspberry jam, for filling
- Optional:
- 2 ounces dark chocolate, coarsely chopped into pieces the size of a quarter and melted (see page 13)

1. Preheat the oven to 350°F with a rack in the center of the oven. Line a baking sheet with parchment.

2. In an extra-large bowl, measure out 8 ounces of the condensed milk by weight. If you don't have a scale, use approximately half of the can. Add the raspberries, vanilla, and lemon zest and combine with a rubber spatula. Add the coconut to the condensed milk mixture and combine until thoroughly mixed.

3. Add the egg whites and salt to the bowl of a stand mixer (or small bowl if you're using a hand beater) and whip on medium-high until very stiff peaks form, 2½ to 3 minutes.

4. Using a rubber spatula, gently fold the egg whites into the coconut mixture. After it's combined, push the mixture into one big blob to make it easier for you to portion out the macaroons.

5. Dip 2 spoons into a small bowl of water, shake them off, form the mixture into balls approximately 1½ inches in diameter, and place them on the baking sheet about 1 inch apart. (You can also form them by hand, but be sure to wet your fingers frequently.)

6. Form a well in the center of each macaroon and spoon jam into the wells. You can either leave them as "thumbprint" cookies or fold up the surrounding macaroon batter to fully enclose the jam. Place the sheet into the oven to bake for 22 minutes. After about 19 minutes, start checking for coloring. Look for an even, light golden color and for the undersides to be nicely tanned.

7. Remove from the oven and transfer the macaroons to a cooling rack to let cool completely, and drizzle with melted chocolate if you'd like. The macaroons will keep at room temperature for 3 to 5 days, for about 3 weeks in an airtight container in the fridge, and for a few months if stored in an airtight container in the freezer.

chocolate macaroon sandwich shells

CHOCOLATE *macaroon* SANDWICH SHELLS

Move over, French macarons! Similar to the original sandwiches, (see page 144), these work with so many different flavors. I particularly love chestnut cream and speculoos spread (not combined, though that's an idea) as filling options.

Yield: Twenty-four 2½-inch macaroon shells (for 12 sandwiches)

MACAROONS:
- One 14-ounce can sweetened condensed milk
- 1 ounce dark chocolate, melted
- ¼ teaspoon vanilla extract
- One 7-ounce bag sweetened shredded coconut
- 1 large egg white
- ¼ teaspoon kosher salt
- Your choice of fillings (see Headnote above)

1. Preheat the oven to 350°F with a rack in the center of the oven. Line 2 baking sheets with parchment.

2. In an extra-large bowl, measure out 5 ounces by weight of the condensed milk. If you don't have a scale, use approximately 4 ounces (½ cup) by liquid measure. Add the melted chocolate and vanilla and incorporate with a rubber spatula. Add the coconut to the condensed milk mixture and combine until thoroughly mixed.

3. Add the egg white and salt to the bowl of a stand mixer (or small bowl if you're using a hand beater) and whip on medium-high until very stiff peaks form, 2½ to 3 minutes.

4. Using a rubber spatula, gently fold the egg white into the coconut mixture. After it's combined, push the mixture into one big blob to make it easier for you to portion out the macaroons.

5. Dip 2 spoons into a small bowl of water, shake them off, form the mixture into balls approximately ¼ inch in diameter, and place them on the baking sheets about 3 inches apart. (You can also form them by hand, but be sure to wet your fingers frequently.)

6. Press out each ball into very thin disks, about 2½ inches in diameter. Place the sheets into the oven to bake for 12 minutes. After about 10 minutes, start checking for coloring. Look for barely darkened edges.

7. Remove from the oven and transfer the macaroons to a rack to cool.

8. Fill with whatever and make them into sandwiches.

9. The macaroons will keep uncovered for 3 to 5 days but for weeks in an airtight container in the fridge, and for who knows how long if stored in the freezer. (This may change depending on what you use for a filling.) If you plan to freeze, consider freezing the shells unfilled.

ORIGINAL *macaroon* SANDWICH SHELLS

Similar to the chocolate sandwiches (see page 142), these go wonderfully well with so many different fillings. I love raspberry or sour cherry jam. Chocolate always works well, as does Key lime curd. Really, it's up to you. Experiment, have fun, create something amazing.

Yield: Twenty-four 2½-inch macaroon shells (for 12 sandwiches)

MACAROONS:

One 14-ounce can
    sweetened condensed milk
½ teaspoon vanilla extract
One 7-ounce bag sweetened
    shredded coconut
1 large egg white
¼ teaspoon kosher salt
Your choice of fillings (see
    Headnote above)

1. Preheat the oven to 350°F with a rack in the center of the oven. Line 2 baking sheets with parchment.

2. In an extra-large bowl, measure out 5 ounces by weight of the condensed milk. If you don't have a scale, use approximately 4 ounces (½ cup) by liquid measure. Add the vanilla and incorporate with a rubber spatula. Add the coconut to the condensed milk mixture and combine until thoroughly mixed.

3. Add the egg white and salt to the bowl of a stand mixer (or small bowl if you're using a hand beater) and whip on medium-high until very stiff peaks form, 2½ to 3 minutes.

4. Using a rubber spatula, gently fold the egg white into the coconut mixture. After it's combined, push the mixture into one big blob to make it easier for you to portion out the macaroons.

5. Dip 2 spoons into a small bowl of water, shake them off, form the mixture into balls approximately ¼ inch in diameter, and place them on the baking sheets about 3 inches apart. (You can also form them by hand, but be sure to wet your fingers frequently.)

6. Press out each ball into very thin disks, about 2½ inches in diameter. Place the sheets into the oven to bake for 12 minutes. After about 10 minutes, start checking for coloring. Look for an even, LIGHT color on top with barely golden edges.

7. Remove from the oven and let the sheets rest on a cooling rack, leaving the macaroons on the sheets until they're cool enough for you to pull off (about 2 minutes depending on how sensitive your fingers are). Transfer the macaroons to the cooling rack to let cool completely.

original macaroon sandwich shells

8. Fill with whatever and make them into sandwiches.

9. The macaroon sandwich shells will keep at room temperature for 3 to 5 days but for weeks and weeks in an airtight container in the fridge, and for up to 6 months if stored in an airtight container in the freezer. (Obviously this may change depending on what you use for a filling.) If you plan to freeze, consider freezing the shells unfilled.

VEGAN *macaroons*

This recipe is very much inspired by the delicious vegan macaroons from Lael Cakes. As I may have mentioned before, there really aren't any rules here, so I deepened the flavor a bit with some molasses and a little bit of brown sugar.

Yield: Twenty-four 2-inch macaroons

MACAROONS:

- One 14-ounce can coconut milk
- One 14-ounce can coconut cream (such as Coco López), shaken or stirred well
- 2 ounces (2½ tablespoons) agave syrup
- 2 tablespoons unsulfured molasses
- 1 tablespoon dark brown sugar
- 1 teaspoon vanilla extract
- ¼ teaspoon kosher salt
- One 14-ounce bag sweetened shredded coconut
- ⅔ cup millet flour

1. Preheat the oven to 350°F with a rack in the center of the oven. Line a baking sheet with parchment.

2. In an extra-large bowl, combine 2 ounces (¼ cup) by liquid measure of the coconut milk, 6 tablespoons of the coconut cream, the agave, molasses, brown sugar, vanilla, and salt and mix thoroughly with a rubber spatula. Add the coconut and millet flour to the coconut milk mixture and combine until thoroughly mixed.

3. Dip 2 spoons into a small bowl of water, shake them off, form the mixture into balls approximately 1½ inches in diameter, and place them on the baking sheet about 1 inch apart. (You can also form them by hand, but be sure to wet your fingers frequently.)

4. Place the sheet into the oven to bake for 20 to 25 minutes. After about 22 minutes, start checking for coloring. Look for an even, light golden color and for the undersides to be nicely tanned.

5. Remove from the oven and let the sheet rest on a cooling rack, leaving the macaroons on the sheet until they're cool enough for you to pull off (about 2 minutes depending on how sensitive your fingers are). Transfer the macaroons to the cooling rack to let cool completely. The macaroons will keep at room temperature for 3 to 5 days, for about 3 weeks in an airtight container in the fridge, and for a few months if stored in an airtight container in the freezer.

INDEX

Page numbers in *italics* indicate illustrations.